Partnerships in Urban Planning

A GUIDE FOR MUNICIPALITIES

Nabeel Hamdi and Michael Majale

Practical Action Publishing Ltd
27a Albert Street, Rugby, CV21 2SG, Warwickshire, UK
www.practicalactionpublishing.org

© Practical Action Publishing Ltd, 2006

ISBN 978 1 85339 657 1 Paperback
ISBN 978 1 78044 152 8 PDF

All rights reserved. No part of this publication may be reprinted or reproduced or utilized in any form or by any electronic, mechanical, or other means, now known or hereafter invented, including photocopying and recording, or in any information storage or retrieval system, without the written permission of the publishers.

A catalogue record for this book is available from the British Library.

The contributors have asserted their rights under the Copyright Designs and Patents Act 1988 to be identified as authors of their respective contributions.

Since 1974, Practical Action Publishing has published and disseminated books and information in support of international development work throughout the world. Practical Action Publishing is a trading name of Practical Action Publishing Ltd (Company Reg. No. 1159018), the wholly owned publishing company of Practical Action. Practical Action Publishing trades only in support of its parent charity objectives and any profits are covenanted back to Practical Action (Charity Reg. No. 247257, Group VAT Registration No. 880 9924 76).

Go to the people
Live among the people
Learn from the people
Plan with the people
Work with the people
Start with what the people know
Build on what the people have
Teach by showing, learn by doing
Not a showcase but a pattern
Not odds and ends but a system
Not piecemeal but integrated approach
Not to confirm but to transform
Not relief but release.

(James Y. C. Yen, founder of the Rural Reconstruction Movement of China, cited in Leyland, 1991:36)

Contents

Acknowledgements .... *vi*

Acronyms and abbreviations .... *vii*

List of boxes, figures and tables .... *viii*

Introduction *1*

Background *1*

Project purpose *2*

Project approach *3*

PART 1 – THE URBAN CHALLENGE *7*

Urbanization and the challenge of urban poverty *7*

Urbanization of poverty *9*

Sustainable urban development *11*

Building the Sustainable City *13*

Participation and partnership: crucial dimensions
for achieving the MDGs *22*

PART 2 – PARTNERSHIPS IN ACTION *25*

Partnerships – What are they? *27*

Purpose of partnerships *29*

Choosing the right partner *32*

Private corporate sector *36*

Building partnerships *37*

Action planning – reaching consensus *45*

PART 3 – GUIDING PRINCIPLES *49*

References *50*

Online resources *54*

Acknowledgements

*This manual is an output of the **Building in Partnership: Participatory Urban Planning Project** which was implemented by the Intermediate Technology Development Group (ITDG) with funding from the UK Government's Department for International Development Knowledge and Research (DFID KaR). The views expressed in the following pages, however, are not necessarily those of DFID.*

The authors would like to acknowledge the valuable work of the wider project team, in particular Paul Chege, the ITDG–EA project manager, who was instrumental in the partnership building process and implementation of project activities in Kitale. Otto Ruskulis compiled the comprehensive reviews of the literature and state-of-the-art of participatory urban planning, which are available on the accompanying CD-ROM along with the case study reports by Saad Yahya (Kenya), Francos Halla (Tanzania), Sarah Ibanda (Uganda), Carlos Frias (Peru), and Satya Ranjan Saha and Habibur Rahman (Bangladesh). The international workshop, which further informed this publication, was facilitated by the superb logistical and administrative support of Susan Yiapan. She, in addition, prepared the workshop report that is also available on the CD-ROM, which was developed and formatted by Ben Pile. The publication layout, design and graphics are the excellent work of Holly Mann.

*Lastly, and most importantly, the authors would like to acknowledge the active participation of Kitale Municipal Council and the citizenry of Kitale town, in particular the residents of Kipsongo, Shimo la Tewa and Tuwani informal settlements, in the **Building in Partnership: Participatory Urban Planning Project** on which this guide is based.*

Acronyms and Abbreviations

ACHR	Asian Coalition for Housing Rights
BiP:PUP	Building in Partnership: Participatory Urban Planning
CBO	Community-based organization
CSO	Civil Society Organization
DFID	Department for International Development
DHSS	Department for Housing and Social Services
ITDG	Intermediate Technology Development Group
ITDG–EA	Intermediate Technology Development Group – Eastern Africa
ITDG–UK	Intermediate Technology Development Group – United Kingdom
KaR	Knowledge and Research
KMC	Kitale Municipal Council
MDGs	Millennium Development Goals
NGO	Non-governmental organization
PRC	Population Resource Center
PVO	Private Voluntary Organization
SDI	Slum/Shack Dwellers International
SL	Sustainable livelihoods
SPARC	Society for the Promotion of Area Resource Centres
UMP	Urban Management Programme
UN	United Nations
UNCHS	United Nations Centre for Human Settlements
UNDP	United Nations Development Programme
UN-ESCAP	United Nations Economic and Social Commission for Asia and the Pacific
ZOPP	Ziel-Orientierte Projekt Planung (Objectives-oriented Project Planning)

List of Boxes, Figures and Tables

Boxes

Box 1	Urban areas, cities and towns	7
Box 2	Slums of the world: a grave and rapidly growing challenge	9
Box 3	Urban poverty	10
Box 4	The 'brown' agenda	13
Box 5	People and governance	16
Box 6	Arguments for and against participation	20
Box 7	Political will	23
Box 8	Definitions of partnership	27
Box 9	What a partnership is not	28

Figures

Figure 1	Urban and rural populations of more developed regions and less developed regions, 1950–2030	8
Figure 2	Cumulative impacts of urban poverty	11
Figure 3	The components of sustainable urban development	12
Figure 4	DFID's Sustainable livelihoods framework	14
Figure 5	Outsiders' control versus local people's control in 7 forms of participation	20
Figure 6	Governance, the idealized model	25
Figure 7	Governance in reality	26
Figure 8	Pursuing an intersectoral agenda	31
Figure 9	Overlapping responsibilities create added complexity: shelter as an example	32
Figure 10	Spatial relation of communities and participatory partners	41
Figure 11	Actors and levels	43
Figure 12	Actors and levels	44

Tables

Table 1	Capital assets	15
Table 2	Aims and tools of good urban governance	17
Table 3	Comparative analysis: participation as means versus end	18
Table 4	Things to consider when deciding on partners	39
Table 5	Factors for success and characteristics of failed partnership	40
Table 6	Stakeholder analysis	41
Table 7	Characteristics of communities as participatory partners	42
Table 8	Actors and levels	43

KITALE, KENYA

Introduction

◆ BACKGROUND

The world as a whole is urbanizing at a rapid pace – but in the developing world, urbanization processes are intensifying at an alarming rate. Three-quarters of global population increase is currently occurring in cities in developing countries. Contemporary rural-urban transformation in Africa, in particular, is taking place in a context of far higher absolute population growth, far lower income levels, and significantly less institutional capacity than was the case during the urbanization of the now-developed world. Consequently, although Africa remains the least urbanized of the continents, it is one region where urbanization is posing perhaps its most difficult challenges (Mabogunje, 2003).

City and municipal authorities in developing countries are facing a considerable challenge as they try to plan and manage the development of cities, and meet their responsibility to deliver services to the citizenry. The problems they face are compounded by the 'urbanization of poverty' – the fact that a rapidly increasing proportion of the world's poor are now living in cities and towns. The proliferation and expansion of slums and informal settlements, in which the growing urban poor majority are compelled to live, are the most conspicuous manifestations of this phenomenon.

A number of factors affect the conditions under which people live and work in urban areas, and how they experience and cope with poverty. Urban centres are characterised by a dense concentration of population, and by the corresponding need for complex delivery systems to meet their resource and service needs (food, water and sanitation, shelter, waste and transport). The competition for space means that housing, a primary asset for the urban poor, and land on which to build are at a premium. On the other hand, density of population provides substantial opportunities, due to economies of scale, for provision of services to poor urban communities. In addition, people's livelihood strategies are dominated by the need for cash to meet their transaction costs (food, rent, utilities, etc.) in a monetised urban economy. Possibilities of earning money, however, provide poor people with more choice in how they sustain and improve their livelihoods (DFID, 2001:13).

If urban dwellers are to enjoy the benefits of living in cities and towns, local authorities must maximise the opportunities offered. This will require effective approaches to urban planning and development and delivery of infrastructure and services.

◆ PROJECT PURPOSE

This guide, with its accompanying CD-Rom, is an output of a three-year project entitled 'Building in Partnership: Participatory Urban Planning' (BiP:PUP). The project was funded by the Department for International Development (DFID) through the Knowledge and Research (KaR) programme. The overall goal of the project was to "Enhance the effectiveness of city and municipal planning and management". More specifically, the project purpose was "To test, develop and disseminate a partnership approach to the planning of urban space with poor men, women, and children, community-based, public, and private organizations".

KITALE, KENYA

The project set out to investigate whether the creation of formal and informal linkages between community-based organizations (CBOs), public agencies and the private sector can build local capacity to assess and meet the needs of urban poor communities. It further sought to test, develop and disseminate methods and approaches to encourage stakeholder participation in assessing needs and developing neighbourhood plans.

The project undertook to achieve the following:

• A worldwide review and synthesis of existing knowledge and methodologies applied in participatory urban planning, particularly in the context of informal settlement development.

• Establishment of linkages and bases for partnerships through participatory baseline surveys and detailed needs assessments.

• Capacity building of project partners to plan and manage the urban built environment locally and influence the approach of the public sector.

• Participatory recording and media coverage of the project process.

• A published methodology for partnership creation and management processes, including tools and techniques.

◆ PROJECT APPROACH

Project activities on the ground were implemented by Intermediate Technology Development Group – Eastern Africa (ITDG-EA) in Kitale, Kenya, while Intermediate Technology Development Group – United Kingdom (ITDG-UK) had overall project management responsibility. A multidisciplinary team used a sustainable livelihoods (SL) approach, participatory urban appraisal methods and community-based indicators to help poor communities in informal settlements define their priorities, plan and implement development activities, and monitor progress.

In the first year of the project, a global review of the literature and current knowledge on participatory planning, particularly in the context of informal settlement development, was conducted (Ruskulis, 2002a; Ruskulis, 2002b; Ruskulis, 2002c). This was intended to inform implementation of project activities on the ground. In addition, consultants undertook case-studies in East Africa – Kenya (Yahya, 2002), Tanzania (Halla, 2002) and Uganda (Ibanda, 2003) – while ITDG–Bangladesh and ITDG–South America carried out case-studies in Bangladesh (Saha, 2003) and Peru (de los Ríos, n.d.) respectively. The case studies were presented at an international workshop in the final year of the project (see below).

Other key first year project activities included preparatory data collection, creation of linkages, and establishment of partnerships and ways of working together. The development of a close working relationship and partnership between ITDG–EA and Kitale Municipal Council (KMC) was a crucial element of the project. As part of the partnership arrangement, the Council provided an office and secretarial support for the ITDG–EA project team within the Town Hall at no cost.

A preliminary scan survey was also carried out, with the Department for Housing and Social Services (DHSS) drawing on its resources and local knowledge and ITDG–EA providing strategic assistance. The purpose of the survey was to identify and map concerns over land tenure, infrastructure (water, sanitation, drainage, solid waste management, and access roads and other footpaths), housing, education, medical services, governance and funding for development projects. The survey was also used to prioritise which of Kitale's ten wards, and more specifically, which informal settlements project, activities would be implemented in. On this basis, three settlements were selected for active intervention through integrative, participatory planning, namely Kipsongo, Tuwan and Shimo La Tewa (see ITDG–EA, 2001c). An inventory of community-based organizations (CBOs) was also conducted to identify ones that were active and that could be involved as partners in the project (ITDG–EA, 2002a).

The project subsequently involved local communities in each of the settlements to identify priority needs (ITDG–EA, 2002d; ITDG–EA, 2002g), and, through a participatory approach, developed neighbourhood plans in Kipsongo (ITDG–EA, 2002d) and Shimo La Tewa (ITDG–EA, 2002f). A community-based planning toolkit was also developed (ITDG–EA, 2001b).

Priorities identified in the participatory neighbourhood planning exercises in Kipsongo and Shimo La Tewa were addressed through funding provided by the project. In Kipsongo, eight sanitation blocks (each comprising two latrines and two bathing cubicles) were built with active community participation; and in Shimo La Tewa, a footbridge was constructed on a cost-sharing basis with KMC, with the local community contributing unskilled labour and a private sector contractor supplying materials at nominal cost. A private sector engineer was also involved in the design and supervision of construction of the footbridge, along with the Municipal Engineer and an engineer from the Ministry of Roads and Public Works.

In the course of project implementation, KMC experienced two major upheavals. In September/October 2001, the Council was dissolved by presidential decree, and the chief officers with whom the project had been engaging were suspended. Then, in December 2002, central and local government elections were held, and the project team had to begin working with a new Mayor and councillors. Having the project office in the Town Hall and, moreover, next to the Mayor's Parlour proved invaluable in re-establishing relationships in both cases.

In the final year of the project, an international workshop was held in Kitale from 9 – 12 June 2003. The purpose of the workshop was to reflect on the case studies and work carried out on the ground, and to draw lessons and make recommendations as a basis for formulating guidance on partnership formation and working. The workshop participants included community representatives from the settlements in which project activities were implemented, KMC staff, other key local stakeholders, the ITDG–EA project team, the authors of the case-studies, the International Project Manager (Michael Majale) and the advisor on the project (Prof. Nabeel Hamdi) (see ITDG–EA, 2003).

An end-of-project evaluation was undertaken in March 2004 to assess the extent to which the project had achieved its purpose: "To test, develop and disseminate a partnership approach to the planning of urban space with poor men, women, and children, community-based, public, and private organizations" – and how far it had moved towards the stated project goal: "To enhance the effectiveness of city and municipal planning and management". The evaluation concluded that:

"The settlements involved have made great strides in terms of physical planning and infrastructure and in terms of their day-to-day management and social structure, and in terms of individuals' capacity...These achievements would not have been possible without heavy involvement of the municipality. However, the municipality would not have been able to undertake such works without the partnership...[KMC's] attitudes to development and to collaboration with the community and external organizations have developed and [it is prepared] to take on a participatory process..." (Lyons, 2004:14).

PART 1 The Urban Challenge

Cities are the engines of growth in the developing world

◆ URBANIZATION AND THE CHALLENGE OF URBAN POVERTY

As the new millennium unfolds, the world is moving rapidly towards 'maximum urbanization'. Simply defined, 'urbanization' is the process of growth in the proportion of people living in urban areas (i.e., the increase in the percentage of a region's population living in urban areas). It is differentiated from 'urban growth' which refers to the proportionate growth of urban areas themselves (i.e., the increase in both the size of the population living in urban areas and the amount of land devoted to urban places) (UNCHS, 1994).

> **Box 1 Urban areas, cities and towns**
>
> *Urban means in or having to do with cities and towns, as distinct from rural areas.*
>
> *A city is an urban area, differentiated from a town by size, population density, importance, or legal status. A city usually consists of residential, industrial and business areas together with administrative functions which may relate to a wider geographical area.*
>
> *In different parts of the world, people might distinguish between towns and cities in a variety of ways. There is no standard international definition of a city: The term may be used either for a town possessing city status, for an urban locality exceeding an arbitrary population size or for a town dominating other towns with particular regional economic or administrative significance.*
>
> *A town is usually an urban locality which is not considered to rank as a city. As with cities, there is no standard definition of a town: the criterion in use in any country is likely to arise from national law, custom or administrative convenience.*
>
> *The distinction between a town and a city similarly depends on the approach adopted: a city may strictly be an administrative entity which has been granted that dignity by law, but the term is also used commonly to denote an urban locality of a particular size or importance. For example, whereas a medieval city may have possessed as few as 10,000 inhabitants, today many would think of an urban place of fewer than 100,000 as a town.*
>
> *A municipality is an administrative local area generally composed of a clearly defined territory and commonly referring to a city or town. In most countries, this is the smallest administrative subdivision that has its own democratically elected representative leadership.*

Source: Wikipedia, the free encyclopedia http://en.wikipedia.org

Part 1 The Urban Challenge

The process of urbanization is already advanced in the more developed regions of the world, where 74 per cent of the population were urban in 2003. Almost all the growth in population between 2000 and 2030 is thus expected to be absorbed by the urban areas of the less developed regions (UN, 2004:2) *(Figure 1)*. The world's population is projected to grow another two billion, to more than eight billion, in the next 30 years, and 95 per cent of this growth will be in the developing world. The almost two billion people presently living in developing world cities will double to four billion by 2030. Approximately 50 per cent of the world's population will consequently be in developing world urban areas, with the associated challenge for developing world national and local governments to provide the necessary infrastructure and services (PRC, 2001).

Although natural population growth is fast becoming a primary causal factor of urban population growth in developing countries, migration from rural to urban areas and the transformation of rural settlements into urban places are important determinants of the anticipated high urban population growth (UN, 2004:1). As 'no country has been effective in restraining rural-urban migration' (World Bank, 1991:18), urban policies and planning need to shift from containing urban growth to guiding and accommodating it.

Figure 1: Urban and rural populations of more developed regions and less developed regions, 1950-2030

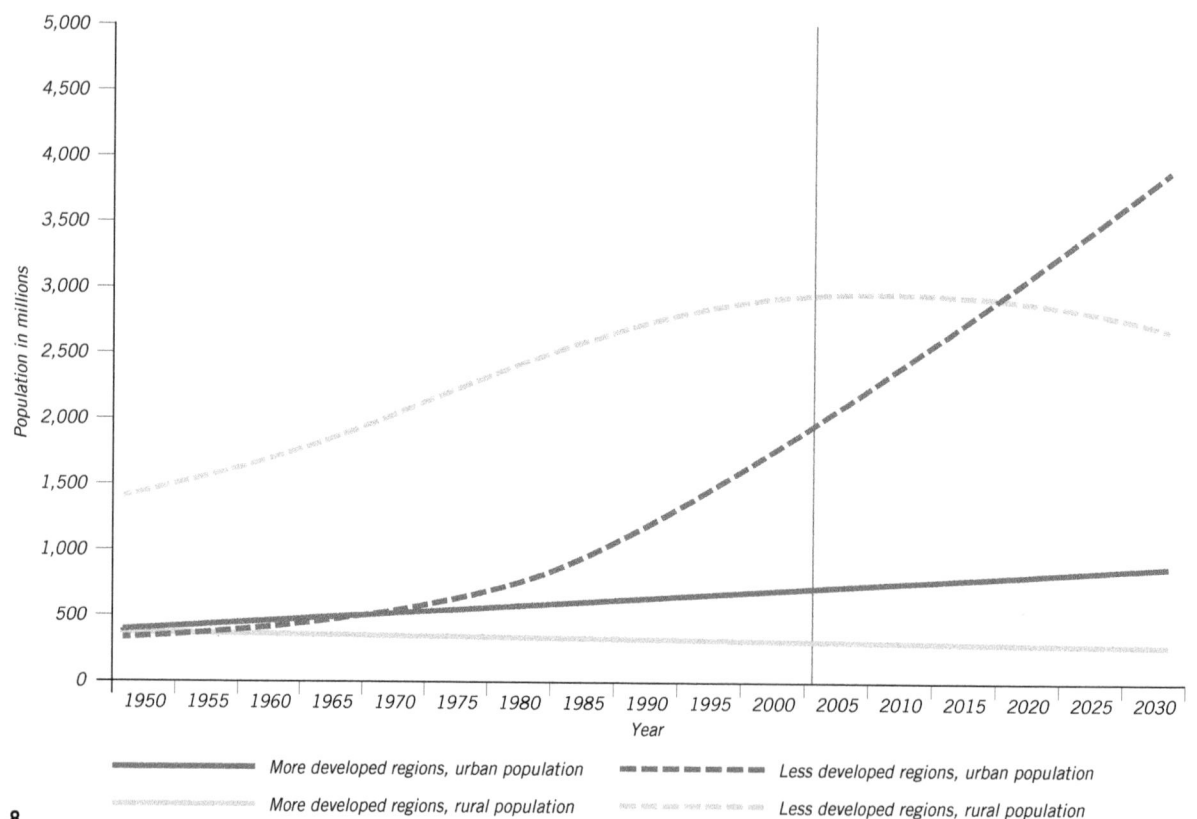

The features of contemporary urbanization in the developing world, however, differ from those experienced earlier in Europe and North America. Urbanization in the latter took many decades, allowing a gradual emergence of economic, social and political institutions to deal with the problems of transformation. The process in developing countries, on the other hand, has been very rapid, against a background of higher population growth rates and lower incomes. The pattern of urbanization in a large proportion of developing countries has also been characterized by a heavy concentration of economic activities and wealth in a few large urban centres (Hassan and Zetter, 2002:16).

Cities in developing countries continue to be built essentially 'back to front' – developing first, with the creation of planning instruments and strategies coming second; building first and servicing last. Yet, despite all its attendant problems, it remains all but impossible to restrain this mode of urban development (Zetter, 2002: 32).

◆ URBANIZATION OF POVERTY

In 1988, the World Bank estimated conservatively that some 330 million people in cities and towns in developing countries were living on less than US $1 a day. In 2000, the estimate had increased to 495 million (Hinrichsen et al, 2002). According to the UNCHS (2001a), 36 per cent of all households and 41 per cent of all women-headed households in urban areas in developing countries live with incomes below the locally defined poverty line. The urbanization and feminization of poverty have thus resulted in over one billion people living in urban areas without adequate shelter or access to basic services.

> **Box 2 Slums of the world: a grave and rapidly growing challenge**
> *There are several important reasons why we need a much sharper focus on the plight of the urban poor:*
>
> *a) The urbanization of the world's population growth. Cities will absorb more than 95 per cent of the world's expected population growth by the year 2030.*
>
> *b) The urbanization of poverty. Given present demographic trends noted above, the majority of the future poor will be urban dwelling.*
>
> *c) The sheer size of the world's slum population. According to the most recent estimates, over 900 million people can be classified as slum dwellers – that is, lacking one or more of the following conditions: access to improved water, access to improved sanitation facilities, sufficient living space, dwellings of sufficient durability and structural quality, security of tenure. In today's world, almost one out of three urban dwellers already lives in a slum.*
>
> *d) The concentration of slum dwellers in the poorest countries. Based on 2001 estimates, 43 per cent of the urban population in the developing regions live in slums.*

Part 1 The Urban Challenge

> *But in the least developed countries, this percentage rises to more than 78 per cent.*
>
> *e) The inequitable and/or life-threatening conditions most slum dwellers live under. Many slums are among the world's most life-threatening environments. In addition, a number of slum dwellers are excluded from the attributes of urban life that remain a monopoly of a privileged minority – political voice, decent housing, safety and the rule of law, education and health, decent transport, adequate incomes.*
>
> *f) Escalating numbers. If present trends continue, 1.5 billion people out of 3.3 billion urban residents will live in slums by the year 2020. However, if policy and structural measures are taken to address this challenge, the incidence of slum dwellers would drop by roughly 700 million individuals – almost exactly halving the number that is predicted if there is no effective change of current trends.*

Source: Garau and Sclar, 2004:1

Statistics alone cannot, however, adequately capture and describe the complexity or diversity of urban poverty *(see Box 3 and Figure 2)*. If urban poverty is to be effectively addressed it needs to be comprehensively understood.

Box 3   Urban poverty

Urban poverty is occasioned (and characterised) by the lack of a secure and sufficient income to provide for the maintenance of a household's livelihood: food, clothing, shelter, health, education and development of each of its members. However, income and wealth (savings) are not the only indices of urban poverty. Such poverty is exacerbated by physical and social insecurity; vulnerability to crises and shocks that may be caused by injury, illness, unemployment, eviction, natural disaster; and ethnic and cultural marginality and ostracism.

Urban poverty impacts upon the poor and undermines the security and efficiency of the whole city. Epidemics originating from unsanitary conditions in slum settlements can spread to all parts of the city, regardless of the income of those affected. Endemic infirmities caused by low levels of nutrition or diseases, such as malaria, seriously reduce the productivity of a city's workforce, as does absenteeism caused by persistent illness. Low levels of education, that result directly from poverty and the lack of schooling opportunities, also have a direct negative impact on the efficiency of commercial and industrial enterprises, as well as the administration of towns and cities. Disparities of wealth, exaggerated by extreme poverty, fuel crime and violence that impinge on all sections of urban society.

The private poverty of individuals fuels the public poverty of towns and cities. Poor urban households are invariably a financial and administrative burden on city administrations. They are net consumers of welfare and environmental services to which they contribute little financially. Thus, it is in the most pragmatic and monetarist interest of urban administrations to reduce poverty, both as a means to lower public costs and to bring poor urban households into the urban economy as tax-paying contributors to the common wealth.

Source: DPU, 2001:3-4

Urban poverty is a multi-dimensional problem and one of the greatest challenges of the New Millennium

Part 1 The Urban Challenge

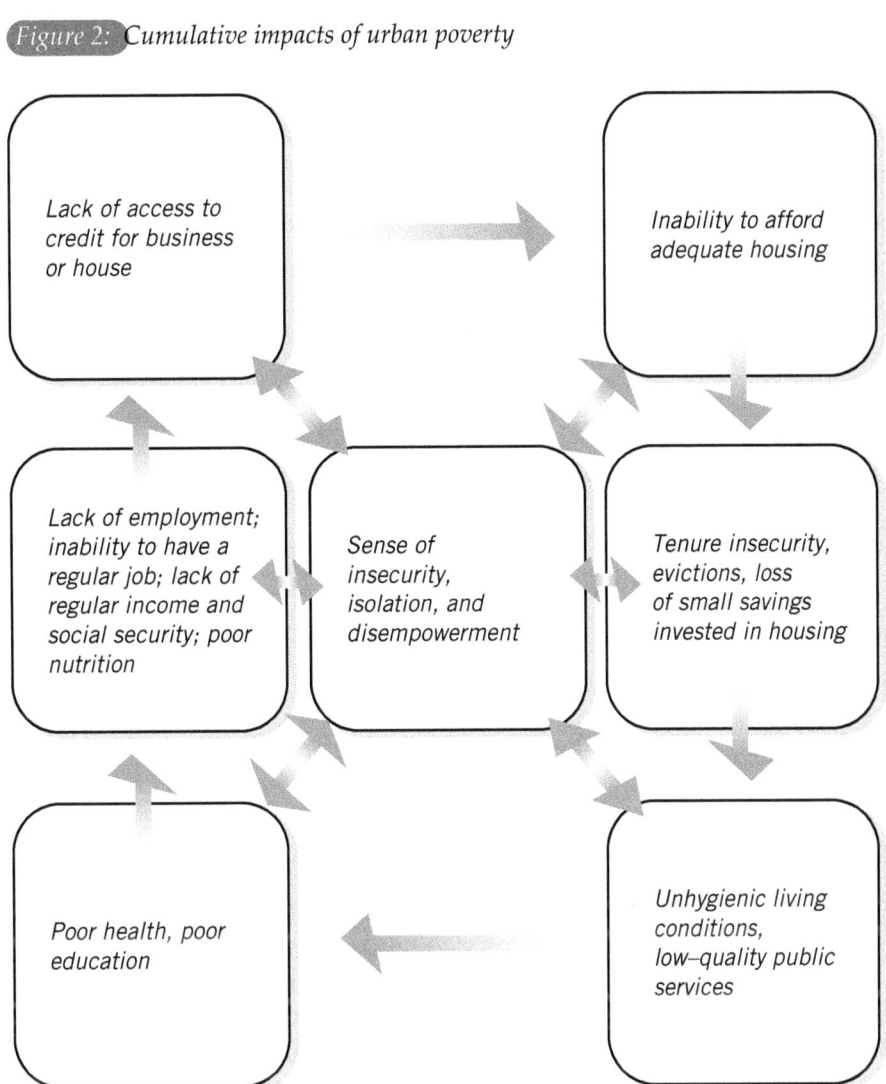

Figure 2: Cumulative impacts of urban poverty

Source: Baharoglu and Kessides, n.d.:127

◆ SUSTAINABLE URBAN DEVELOPMENT

City and municipal authorities have historically been concerned with the economic and social growth and sustainability of their communities. They have also played a foremost role in ensuring better environments for their communities. Local authorities develop, operate and maintain economic, social and environmental infrastructure, oversee planning processes, and establish local environmental policies and regulations. And as the level of government closest to the people, they play a vital role in educating, mobilising and responding to the public to promote sustainable urban development (UNCED, 1992) *(see Figure 3).*

Part 1 *The Urban Challenge*

Figure 3: *The components of sustainable urban development*

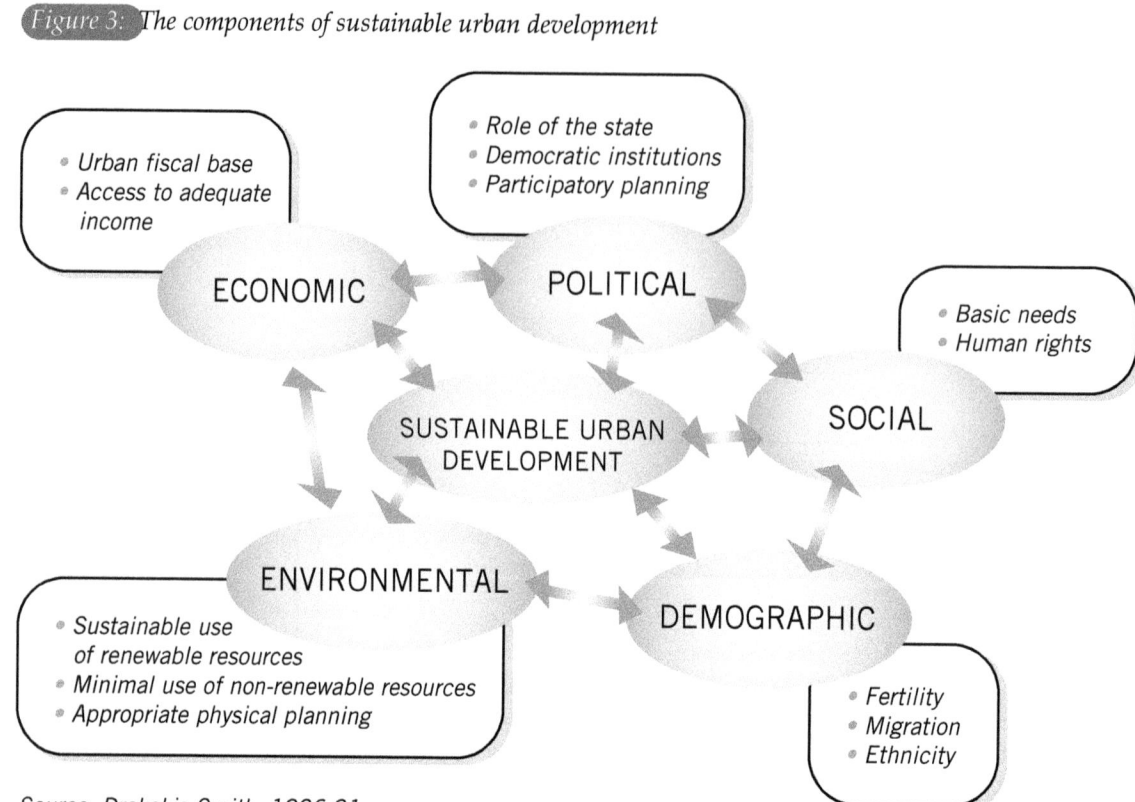

Source: Drakakis-Smith, 1996:31

What is 'sustainable urban development'? The concept of sustainable urban development, as articulated by Drakakis-Smith (1996:30-2), has both a macro-dimension in that it should encompass a philosophical approach and policy and management issues, and a micro dimension in that it should identify the major components of what might constitute a comprehensive programme of sustainable urban development. At the micro-level, the areas of concern (which should be addressed in an integrative manner as they are interconnected), include:

•   Economic activities – employment and poverty. The role of the informal sector is undoubtedly important in this context.

•   The physical urban environment itself – the so called 'brown agenda' *(see Box 4)*.

•   The social urban environment – which is more commonly thought of as basic needs provision, encompassing a very wide range of concerns, from shelter to food, education and health care. There are clearly opportunities for sustainable urban development though co-operation and partnership between the individual (household) and the state (local and central government) in meeting basic needs.

- The demographic situation – it is evident that cities are growing more rapidly than overall populations, but the nature of that growth needs to be carefully assessed and incorporated into development planning and decision making.

- The political sphere – in addition to being an important dimension of urban sustainability, for example though the need for a planning process that fully incorporates the poorer elements of society, it overlaps, as a concept, into urban management as a practical process. It is urban and national politics that determines, to a large extent, the sustainability of urban development.

Box 4 The 'brown' agenda
The 'brown' agenda are sanitary and environmental health issues, which include unsanitary living conditions, hazardous pollutants in the urban air and waterways, and accumulations of solid waste. Such problems have many immediate environmental health impacts which tend to fall especially heavily on the urban poor. The more recent 'green' agenda, promoted by environmentalists (mostly from high-income countries), includes issues such as the contribution of urban-based production, consumption and waste generation to ecosystem disruptions, resource depletion, and global climate change. Most such problems have impacts that are more delayed and dispersed, and often threaten long-term ecological sustainability.

Source: McGranahan and Satterthwaite, 2002:43

The combination of the pace and scale of urban population growth in developing countries is undermining the efforts of city and municipal administrations to achieve sustainable urban development though formulating and implementing appropriate planning and regulatory mechanisms, and providing infrastructure, housing, and other social services such as health, education and security. Their frustrations are further compounded by increasing urban poverty.

Sustainable urban growth is central to sustainable world development

◆ BUILDING THE SUSTAINABLE CITY

In seeking to tackle the multi-dimensional phenomenon of urban poverty and achieve sustainable urban development, city and municipal authorities should take into consideration various themes and issues, including those below.

Sustainable livelihoods

A 'sustainable livelihoods' (SL) approach is a valuable way of understanding and responding to the complexity of the livelihoods of the urban poor. Moreover, it offers a comprehensive insight into the multiple dimensions of poverty for the purposes of city/town and municipal planning. Conceptually, 'livelihoods' connotes the means, activities, entitlements and assets by which people make a living. The sustainability of livelihoods, therefore, is a function of how members of a society utilize assets to meet their needs without compromising the needs of future generations (UNDP, n.d.:2).

SL frameworks are diagrammatic tools intended to improve understanding of livelihoods. They help to illustrate various factors which enhance or constrain livelihood opportunities, and to show how they relate to each other. In the SL framework developed by DFID *(see Figure 4)*, people are seen as pursuing livelihoods in a vulnerability context, where they are exposed to external shocks and stresses. The vulnerability context includes population trends, resource trends (including conflict), national/international economic trends, trends in governance (including politics), technological trends, human health shocks, natural shocks, economic shocks, conflict, crop/livestock health shocks, and seasonality of prices, production, health and employment opportunities. Within this context they have access to various livelihood assets – natural capital, physical capital, human capital, financial capital and social capital *(see Table 1)*. This environment also influences people's livelihood strategies, that is, the ways in which they combine and use assets in pursuit of livelihood outcomes. The viability and effectiveness of livelihood strategies is dependent upon the availability and accessibility of assets which in turn is positively or adversely affected by policies, institutions and processes.

Figure 4: DFID's Sustainable livelihoods framework

Key:
H = Human Capital
S = Social Capital
N = Natural Capital
P = Physical Capital
F = Financial Capital

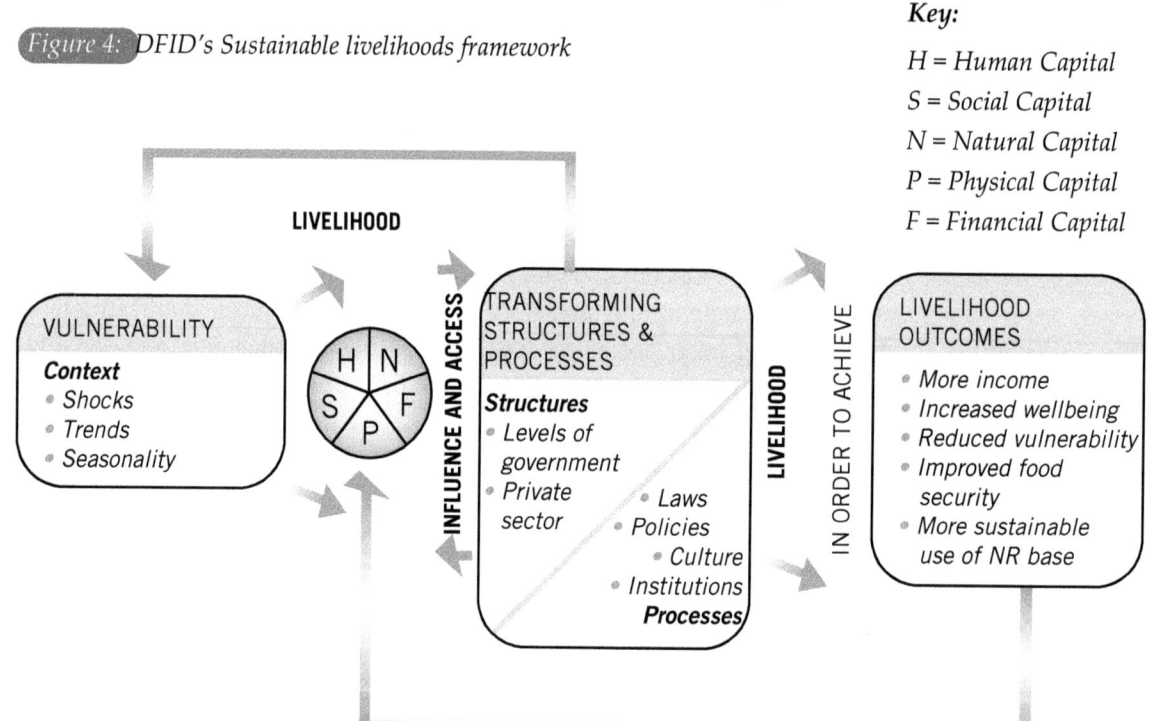

Source: Adapted from Ashley and Carney, 1999:47

> **Table 1: Capital Assets**
>
> *Natural capital:* the natural resource stocks from which resource flows useful for livelihoods are derived, e.g. land, water, bio-diversity, environmental resources.
>
> *Social capital:* the social resources (relationships of trust, membership of groups, networks, access to wider institutions) upon which people draw in pursuit of livelihoods.
>
> *Human capital:* the knowledge, skills, ability to labour, information and good health important to the ability to pursue different livelihoods.
>
> *Physical capital:* the basic infrastructure (water, sanitation, energy, transport, communications), housing and the means and equipment of production.
>
> *Financial capital:* the financial resources which are available to people (savings, credit, regular remittances or pensions) and which provide them with different livelihood options.

Governance

The concept of "governance" is not new – it is as old as human civilization. Simply put, "governance" is 'the process of decision-making and the process by which decisions are implemented (or not implemented)'. Governance can be used in several contexts such as international governance, national governance, local governance or corporate governance. If governance is the process of decision-making and the process by which decisions are implemented, an analysis of governance should focus on the formal and informal actors involved in decision-making and implementing the decisions made and the formal and informal structures that have been set in place to arrive at and implement the decision (UN-ESCAP, n.d.). Government is one of the actors in governance; other actors involved in governance will vary depending on the level of government (*see Table 2 and Box 5*).

Improved urban governance is one of the most important factors in reaching the potential of cities, both in harnessing economic opportunities and in addressing the challenge of urban poverty (UMP, 2001). Indeed, the underlying message in the Habitat Agenda (UNCHS, 1997) is that 'good urban governance, which entails transparency, accountability, popular participation and partnerships, is a precondition for the achievement of sustainable urban development and adequate shelter for all' (Jurra, 2001).

Box 5 People and Governance

Governance is much more than government. At the city level, it can be defined as the sum of the ways through which individuals and institutions (public and private) plan and manage their common affairs. It is a continuing process that may either lead to conflict or to mutually beneficial cooperative action. It includes formal institutions and informal arrangements, as well as the social capital of citizens.

Effective governance is increasingly dependent on people assuming their responsibilities as citizens and participating in decision-making and implementation. Citizens are learning to forge new alliances that strengthen their voice and make their concerns felt in legislation hitherto dominated by private interests. People may form collective entities or groups around common goals, becoming stronger political voices in the process. For their part, governments at all levels increasingly recognize the value of communication and consultation, negotiation of joint decisions and joint implementation of policies in meeting the changing needs of civil society.

Participation is often needed to define, elaborate and implement policies that are more responsive to community problems and needs. Participation can also contribute to better provision of goods and services, especially in cities where public institutions are unable or unwilling to provide them.

Source: UNCHS, 2001b:90

Good urban governance is a prerequisite to sustainable urban development and urban poverty reduction. With developing country cities unable to provide basic infrastructure and services for their citizens, effective decentralization, efficient management of limited resources, popular participation and the development of productive partnerships between the city and the state, civil society, grassroots communities, as well as the private sector, are essential tools in the fight against urban poverty (UN-Habitat, n.d.).

Participation

'Participation' has various meanings and practices. The meanings are often indistinct – and there are different interpretations of the framework of 'participation'. However, in this context it can be interpreted in two broad ways: as a means (instrumental participation) to improve development activities (i.e. making the interventions more effective and sustainable by involving the users or as an end in itself) or ensuring people's influence on their own situation as empowerment (transformational participation) (Buch-Hansen, 2002). These two definitions, which are neither exact nor mutually exclusive, represent two different purposes and approaches to promoting participatory development (UNDP, 1998), and are summarised in Table 3 on page 24.

People are a nation's greatest resource

Table 2: Aims and tools of good urban governance

Aim	Tools
Greater local participation and involvement	• Promotion of city identity and sense of citizenship for all • Public meetings, participatory planning and budgeting • City referenda and public petitioning • Better democratic structures and culture • Involvement of marginalised groups in the city systems
Efficient urban management	• Taking account of all interests in promoting efficiency and better services • Labour relations • Efficient investment in infrastructure • Delegation of decision taking to the lowest appropriate level • Collaboration and partnerships, rather than competition • Appropriate training to improve capacity of city officials • Using information technology to best advantage • Environmental planning and management carried out in co-operation with the citizens • Disaster preparedness and crime control for safer environments
Accountability/ transparency	• Monitoring of government activities by coalitions of outside organizations • Rigorous accounting procedures • Clear guidelines on conduct for leaders and officials that are enforced • Open procurement and contracting systems • Transparency in financial arrangements • Disclosure of information • Fair and predictable regulatory frameworks • Independent and accessible complaints procedures • Regular flow of information on key issues • A wide range of suppliers
Accessibility	• Regular and structured consultation with representative bodies from all sectors of society • Including individuals in the decision-making processes • Access to government by all individuals and organizations • Access to economic opportunity • Protection of the rights of all groups

Source: The Global Urban Development Research Centre, http://www.gdrc.org/u-gov/aim-tool.html

Table 3: Comparative Analysis: Participation as Means versus End

Participation as Means	Participation as End
• It implies use of participation to achieve some predetermined goal or objective.	• Participation as an end attempts to empower people to participate in their own development more meaningfully.
• It is an attempt to utilise the existing resources in order to achieve the objective of programmes/projects.	• The attempt is to ensure the increased role of people in development initiatives.
• The stress is on achieving the objective and not so much on the act of participation itself.	• The focus is on improving the ability of the people to participate rather than just in achieving the predetermined objectives of the project.
• It is more common in government programmes e.g. where the main concern is to mobilise the community and involve them in improving the efficiency of the delivery system.	• This view finds relatively less favour with the government agencies. NGOs in principle agree with this viewpoint.
• Participation is generally short-term.	• Participation as an end is viewed as a long-term process.
• Participation as a means, therefore, appears to be a passive form of participation.	• Participation as an end is relatively more active and dynamic.

Source: Oakley et al., 1991

An alternative way of distinguishing between different forms of participation is to think in terms of degrees or levels of participation. These can be understood along a continuum that ranges from participation as essentially an act of manipulation to a level of participation in which stakeholders become partners in a development initiative and begin to assume full responsibility for its management (UNDP, 1998):

(i) *Manipulation*: the lowest degree applies to situations of 'non-participation', where participation is taken as an opportunity to indoctrinate.

(ii) *Information*: when stakeholders are informed about their options, rights and responsibilities the first important step towards real participation takes place.

The main shortcoming at this stage is that emphasis is placed on one-way communication, with neither channels for feedback nor power for negotiation.

(iii) *Consultation*: which entails two-way communication, where stakeholders have the opportunity to offer suggestions and express concerns, but with no assurance that their input will be used at all or as they intended.

(iv) *Consensus-building*: where stakeholders interact in order to understand each other and arrive at negotiated positions which the entire group can tolerate. A common shortcoming is that vulnerable individuals and groups tend to remain silent or passively agree.

(v) *Decision-making*: when consensus is acted upon through collective decisions, marking the beginning of shared responsibilities for outcomes that may result.

(vi) *Risk-sharing*: which encompasses the effects of decision-making – a mix of beneficial, harmful, and natural consequences. As things are constantly in flux, there is always the element of risk, where even the best intended decisions may yield the least desired results. Accountability is essential at this level, especially when those with the greatest leverage may be the ones with the least at risk.

(vii) *Partnership*: entails exchange among equals working towards a mutual goal. Equal, as applied here, is not in terms of form, structure, or function but rather in terms of balance of respect. Since partnership builds upon the preceding levels, it assumes mutual responsibility and risk sharing.

(viii) *Self-management*: is the pinnacle of participatory efforts, where stakeholders interact in learning processes which optimise the well-being of all concerned.

Participation can also be viewed in terms of outsiders' control versus local people's control *(see Figure 5)*:

There is significant evidence that participation can, in many circumstances improve the quality, effectiveness and sustainability of projects, and strengthen ownership and commitment of government and stakeholders. Community participation strategies are found to be especially important in reaching the poor (World Bank, 1994:i). While there are strong supportive arguments for participation, there are also associated risks *(see Box 6)*.

Figure 5: Outsiders' control versus local people's control in 7 forms of participation

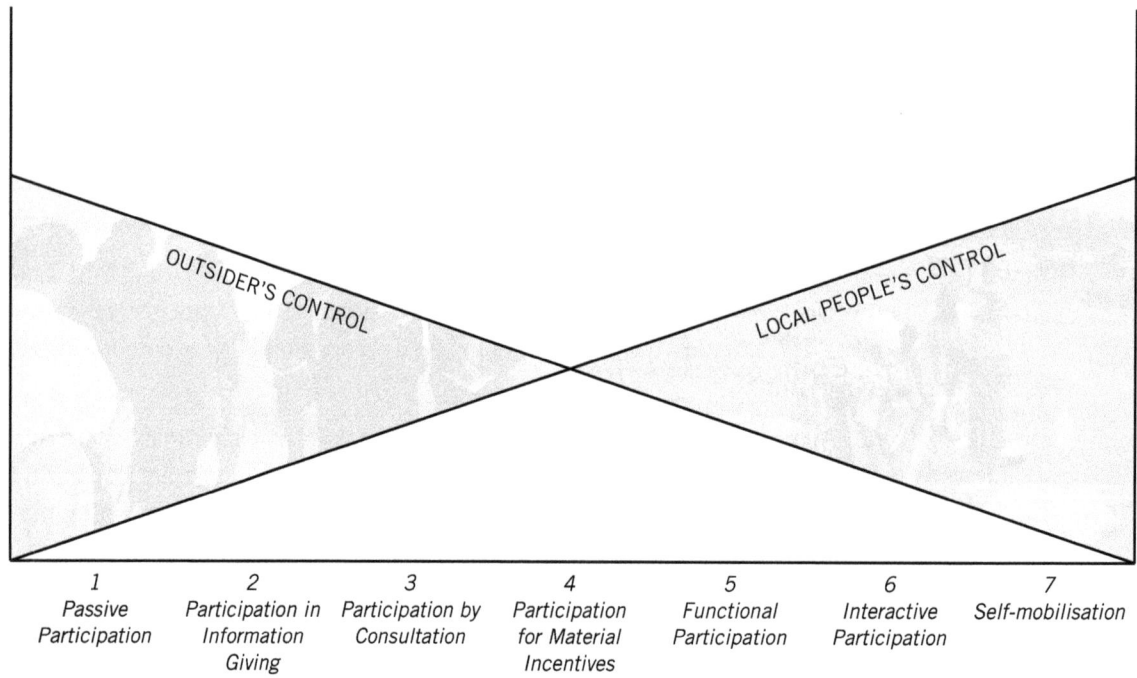

1	2	3	4	5	6	7
Passive Participation	Participation in Information Giving	Participation by Consultation	Participation for Material Incentives	Functional Participation	Interactive Participation	Self-mobilisation

Source: Buch-Hansen, 2002:5

Box 6 Arguments for and against participation
Benefits of participation

○ People's participation can **increase the efficiency** of development activities by mobilizing local resources and skills.

○ Participation can increase coverage when it **mobilizes local resources** and thus helps to extend the range of activities of a development initiative.

○ It can also increase the effectiveness of development activities by ensuring that activities are based on local knowledge and understanding of problems and will be more **relevant to local needs**.

○ Participation can lead to **better targeting of benefits** to the poorest via the identification of key stakeholders and their involvement in subsequent stages of the project or policy work.

○ Participation can often help to improve the status of women by providing the opportunity for them to play a part in development work.

○ Participation helps **build local capacities** and develop the abilities of local people to manage and to negotiate development activities partly through learning by doing.

○ Participation can be crucial in helping to secure the sustainability of the activities as **beneficiaries assume ownership**, which is critical for maintaining momentum.

Risks associated with participation

○ Participation costs **time** and **money** and there is no guaranteed impact upon the end product. Participation can greatly add to the costs of a development activity and therefore its benefits have to be carefully calculated.

○ Processes of participation may be irrelevant and a **luxury** in emergencies or situations of poverty. It may be hard to justify expenditure on such a process where people need first to be fed and their livelihoods secured.

○ Participation can be a **destabilizing force** in that it can unbalance existing socio-political relationships and threaten the continuity of development work.

○ Participation can result in the **shifting of the burden** onto the poor and the relinquishing by national governments of their responsibilities to promote development with equity.

○ Participation is **difficult to plan**: its course is not foreseeable since community decisions are not always predictable.

○ Difficulties which have been encountered in participatory projects include **delays in implementation**, and **over dependence on charismatic project leaders**.

○ The risk of abuse by individuals, local elites or interest groups has to be borne in mind.

Source: SURF-AS, 1999:2-3

Barriers to effective participation

○ **Lack of opportunity** – Apart from voting in national and city elections every few years, most city dwellers have no further opportunities to engage in any aspect of city government.

○ **Lack of time** – Poor city residents are so busy trying to earn and support themselves that they have little time and energy to participate, even when opportunities are available.

○ **Dependency** Government services and benefits are seen as favours rather than rights. This helps to increase dependency of poor people on the government and to erode local decision-making.

○ **Political pressures** – Many elected leaders act as gatekeepers to information, opinions and decisions rather than sharing them openly with the community. Some base their decisions and patronage on personal or political interests.
People without links or connections do not feel represented by these leaders.

Source: CARE, 2001:7

◆ PARTICIPATION AND PARTNERSHIP: CRUCIAL DIMENSIONS FOR ACHIEVING THE MDGs

The Millennium Development Goals (MDGs) offer a comprehensive agenda for reducing the causes and manifestations of poverty by 2015 (Bonfiglioli, n.d.:1). The MDGs are a set of development objectives, the achievement of which requires conducive policy frameworks, sufficient resources and enabling institutional environments – all important governance issues. The realization of the MDGs is fundamentally dependent upon good governance, which encompasses participation and partnership. All these issues are especially important in new or restored democracies, with all their serious economic, social and political problems. The achievement of the MDGs in such situations will require even more effort, stronger commitment and bonded partnerships (Jahan, 2003:4).

At least five reasons can be put forward as to why participation and partnership are crucial for the achievement of the MDGs (Jahan, 2003:4):

- First, MDGs represent the commitment of every country and the entire world to objectives which reflect some core human values. MDGs affect every life on the planet and every one of us should participate in the process that influences its direction, nature and success. As a Brazilian farmer said, if poverty is halved in 2015, I would like to make sure that I am in the right half.

- Partnership is necessary for MDGs as the goals represent too big and too complex a task to be left to one development actor. Partnership brings actors, even those who have traditionally held opposing views, together and contributes to a unifying force for MDGs.

- One major contribution of partnership is that various partners with their diverse expertise and experience bring different value-added to the process, which creates a strong synergy in initiatives towards achieving MDGs. For example, civil society, because of its grassroots work and experience of movements, brings to the process participation by common people, a touch of realism, a demand for transparency and accountability.

- Partnership can also bring sectoral coherence as various actors work in diverse sectors. Partnership provides a forum within which relationships are formed, which could then improve intra- and inter-sectoral coherence and coordination towards attaining the MDGs.

- Due to the long-term nature of the MDGs, partnerships may result in on-going and equal relationships over a longer period of time. Such compacts have externalities in terms of building social capital and enhancing social cohesion, which can also be beneficial to society through other initiatives as well.

In particular, meeting MDG 7, Target 11 – "Achieve, by 2020, a significant improvement in the lives of at least 100 million slum dwellers"– will require that the poor be given a stronger voice in all aspects of planning and governance. It will demand strong political will (UN-Habitat, 2003:2). This will entail an institutional environment that permits forward thinking and partnership among local communities, government, NGOs and the private sector (World Bank, 2003).

> **Box 7 Political will**
> *The most important factor that limits progress in improving housing and living conditions of low-income groups in informal settlements and slums is the lack of genuine political will to address the issue in a fundamentally structured, sustainable and large-scale manner. There is no doubt that the political will to achieve long lasting and structured interventions constitutes the key to success, particularly when accompanied by local ownership and leadership, and the mobilization of the potential and capacity of all the stakeholders, particularly the people themselves. Lessons from several countries underscore the fundamental role of sustained political will and commitment in improving or reducing slums.*

Source: UN-Habitat, 2003:5-6

KITALE, KENYA

Part 2 Partnerships in Action

When it comes to managing urban shelter, services and utilities, conventional wisdom accepts that the way forward is in partnership usually between some form of public and private entity. The term 'partnership', however is ambiguous in various ways.

- It implies relationships based on mutual trust, fairness, equity, respect, accountability, shared values, and shared aspirations which are often subjective, difficult to quantify and most times difficult to find in practice (Brinkerhoff, 2002:14).

- Partnership often refers to a relationship between sectors (public, private, community) that are idealised and in their own right abstractions. Figure 6 below illustrates idealized relationships often promoted in today's emphasis on good governance between the state, the market and the community. These are often considered to be homogenous. Relationships are assumed to be equidistant in terms of communication, equal in size and power, with strong and well-established links. Figure 7 is more representative. It highlights the need amongst constituent partners for capacities to be enhanced, links to be established or strengthened, and power to be shared.

Figure 6: Governance, the idealized model

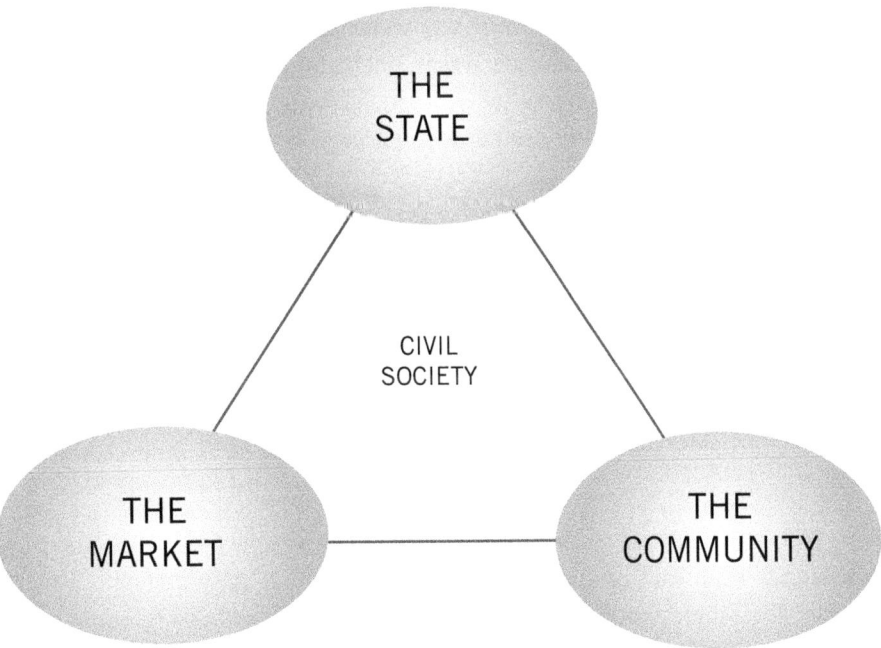

Figure 7: Governance in reality

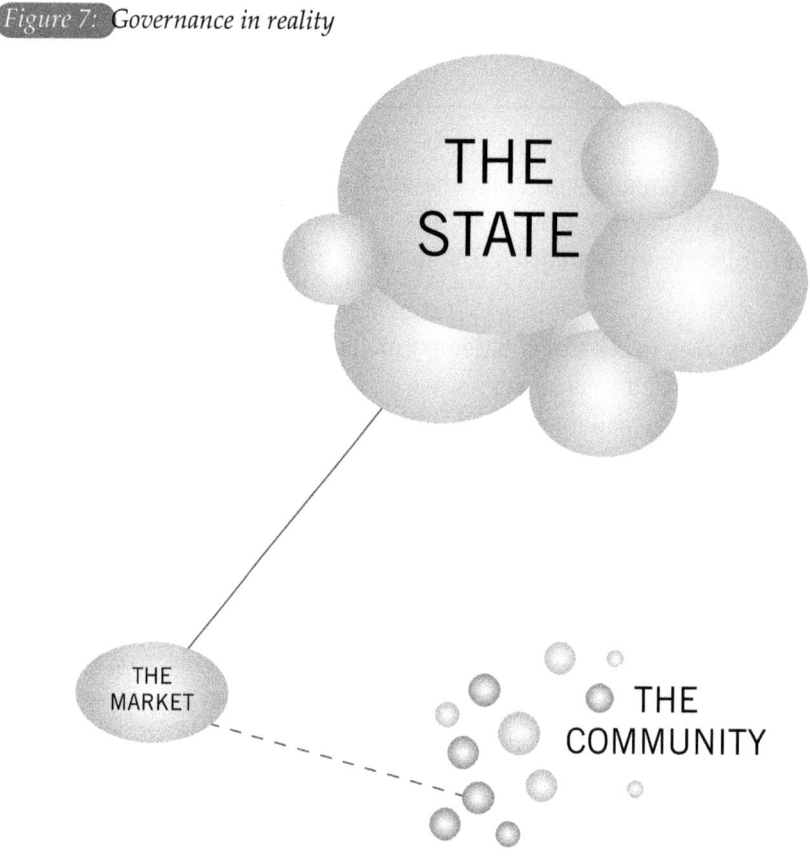

- The search for best practice gives precedent to the idea that partnerships, like projects, that have worked well in one place can be replicated elsewhere. Experience suggests, however, that often these blueprints will fail or be unacceptable because of differences in power relations, social acceptability or political readiness between partners.

- The purpose of partnership like participation is sometimes ambiguous in terms of means and ends (Brinkerhoff 2002:17). As an end it is often an expression of shared values, a commitment to co-operation in pursuit of ideals For example, empowerment, social ownership, community mobilisation. NGOs are often at the forefront of the 'ends' position. As a means, partnerships are instrumental at meeting operational objectives. They are an effective way of improving the efficiency of urban systems in the context of under-resourced municipalities and the growing complexity of delivering and managing urban services.

- More often means and ends converge in themes such as good governance, livelihood security and social enterprise development. For example "social enterprises offer ways of involving excluded groups in designing and delivering their own services... They enable local residents to develop skills, self-confidence, business experience and employability... They aim to build a long term business (means) with a clear focus on community (end)".

Given these issues, what are some of the key principals that underpin good partnerships? What purpose do they serve and for whom? Who are the actors and what is their vested interest? What are their advantages and risks? What criteria should be applied when deciding on partners?

◆ PARTNERSHIPS – WHAT ARE THEY?

'Partnership' is one of those words with multiple and ambiguous meanings (Boyle, n.d.:4). A partnership may be a means of 'getting people together' to begin a debate or share information, a contractually-based arrangement for service delivery, or it may even be a policy-making forum (Lowndes, 2001).

> **Box 8 Definitions of partnership**
>
> Poole (1995:2) defines partnership as: 'an association between two or more persons, groups, or organizations who join together to achieve a common goal that neither one alone can accomplish. This association is characterized by joint membership rights, by democratic participation, and by shared responsibility. Each member agrees to contribute resources to the partnership with the understanding that the possession or enjoyment of the benefits will be shared by all. Partners work hard to strengthen each other and to endure conflict and change, because they recognize that their shared goal extends beyond the reach of any one member.'

Partnering is defined by Demirjian (2002:5) as "an agreed-upon arrangement between two or more parties to work collaboratively toward shared objectives – an arrangement in which there is (i) sharing of work, responsibility and accountability; (ii) joint investment of resources; (iii) shared risk-taking; and (iv) mutual benefits".

Whatever the definition, consensus suggests the following four key elements which distinguish and define partnerships:

- common objectives and goals among partners (objectives may be the impetus of the partnership or they may evolve over time);
- shared risk and mutual benefits (risks and benefits may be different for each partner and may accrue with different time frames);
- contributions from all partners (both monetary and non-monetary)
- shared authority, responsibility and accountability.

Underlying several of the definitions is the notion that the partnership represents, to all partners, a better strategy to address a specific project or goal than each partner operating independently (Ekos, 1998).

Box 9 What a partnership is not

There is a bit of confusion about what is or is not a partnership.
Although a name is just a name, generally a true partnership does not exist when:

- there is simply a gathering of people who want to do things;
- there is a hidden motivation;
- there is an appearance of common ground but actually many agendas exist;
- there is tokenism, or the partnership was established just for appearances;
- one person has all the power and/or drives the process; or
- there is no sharing of risk, responsibility, accountability and benefits.

Source: Frank and Smith, 2000:6

There are no text book partnerships: each will assume its own characteristics, functions, jurisdictions and parameters. Nor are partnerships neat, tidy or predictable (Frank and Smith, 2000:73).

Brinkerhoff suggests two defining dimensions of partnerships – mutuality and organizational identity.

Mutuality entails co-operation between key stakeholders – a partnership between vested interest groups – a context in which users become partners in a social enterprise that can include state and private organizations as well as donors and CBOs. It entails an arrangement where talents, skills or know how is exchanged amongst partners for the benefit of all.

Mutuality builds on the strengths of each party within limits and agreements set by all partners. It accepts that all parties, however unequal in experience, talent, or power, represent an asset and are responsive to each other's needs. It entails a strong commitment to partnership goals that at the outset will have been negotiated and prioritised. Mutuality moves relationships from a hierarchical state of dependence and independence toward one that is horizontal and interdependent. It is a state where users become partners and where "all parties have an opportunity to influence their shared objectives, processes, outcomes and evaluations..." (Brinkerhoff 2002:15).

The second defining dimension is identity. The issue here is the double identity demanded of actors in any given partnership that gives them both distinction and legitimacy. There is the identity of each individual partner organization, whether it be community based or private enterprise. Then there is the common identity established by the collective and in pursuit of common goals. As Brinkerhoff (2002:15) points out, "The creation and maintenance of organizational identity is essential to long term success. Successful

"Mutuality entails an arrangement where talents, skills, or know how is exchanged amongst partners for the benefit of all."

organizations do not maintain organizational systems, processes and strategies as much as they maintain continuity of core beliefs and values across time and contexts. In fact, successful organizations change in response to turbulent environments precisely in order to maintain their identity over time."

"...successful organizations change in response to turbulent environments precisely in order to maintain their identity over time."

Brinkerhoff goes on to suggest two levels at which identity needs to be defined and examined. First a commitment to the partnership mission, core values, and constituencies – that is those stakeholders who are legitimate who have signed up to the mission of the whole, and who recognise mutual advantage of partnership. Second, there is the identity of each individual constituent who's expertise, skills, code of conduct and shared behaviour enables it at once to be distinct from and yet integral to the whole. The loss of distinction leads to dependence; the loss of commitment to the whole leads to competition and undermines the values and effectiveness of the whole.

Both mutuality and identity are essential to the function of partnerships and important to their continuity and relevance over time.

◆ PURPOSE OF PARTNERSHIPS

Partnerships offer various advantages to stakeholders (as well as risks). These risks and advantages provide a first basis for deciding the appropriateness and subsequently the form the partnership might take.

Partnerships offer the opportunity to create organizations which, once established, share the rewards and risks of designing, implementing and managing urban shelter, services and utilities (water trusts, housing co-operatives, re-cycling enterprises). More recently and more typically in development work, partnerships are a basis from which to build a network or federated organization – to advocate causes, promote rights, share knowledge, or provide technical assistance (for example, Peoples Dialogue, Asian Coalition for Housing Rights (ACHR), Homeless International).

Some of the more common advantages include:
Mutual gain/access to resources – Resources may not be available within any one partner organization and where the pooling of resources offers added value. In this sense partnerships help rationalise resources and skills because each party can do what it knows how to do best with consensus on aims and yet without compromise to efficiency. As Birkerhoff says: "the primary driver of partnerships is the need to access resources, to achieve objectives when those resources are lacking or insufficient within one actor's reserves. Such assets can include hard resources, such as money and materials, as well as important soft resources like managerial and technical skills, information, contacts, and credibility within a specialised area."

A key to scaling up impact – Partnerships offer a multiplier effect both in terms of access to resources and also in scaling up the size of the organisation to match the size of the problem or task at hand. Community based Waste Pickers for example in partnership with other Waste Pickers city wide, can make a significant impact on improving waste management. When partnered with private sector paper, glass or plastics manufacturers, the result is both an improvement to the livelihoods of Waste Pickers and to the environment locally, nationally, even globally.

Promotes good governance, arguing for transparency, accountability and democratisation of decision making – Good governance offers new incentives for partnership between the state, the market and community-based organizations. A mediating role for civil society is re-affirmed. The debate on governance acknowledges advantages inherent in the multiplicity of actors and the diversity of their skills working in cities at the local level, using and providing goods and services. It seeks to engage these as partners in 'co-production' for mutual gain.

Offers practical incentives to decentralise which is recognised as integral to good governance – "Decentralisation has created the potential for both partnerships and government partners at the local level… Decentralisation is essential to enhancing not just efficiency and effectiveness but also participation and responsiveness." (Birkerhoff, 2002:28) As Brinkerhoff suggests there are three ways in which decentralisation is conducive to partnerships:

(i) *administrative decentralisation* which enables authorities to respond easily to needs on the ground;

(ii) *financial decentralisation* which facilitates the selection of projects and programmes which financially support local partners; and

(iii) *political decentralisation*, transferring accountability and decision making to local people and organizations.

Pursuing an inter-sectoral agenda – Urban projects and programmes targeted at meeting the Millennium Development Goals demand both sectoral work (housing, water, sanitation, education, health etc.) which integrates intersectoral themes in the interests of longer term development goals (for example social development, regulatory reform, environmental sustainability, enhanced livelihoods, promoting rights, gender awareness) *(see Figure 8)*. This requires co-operation and co-ordination between authorities, community groups, NGOs and sometimes private sector partners. Intersectoral partnerships between, for example municipal authorities, between NGOs and between municipal authorities and NGOs are complex in an environment where authorities and NGOs compete for resources and sometimes political status, and where results are not easy to measure.

Figure 8: Pursuing an intersectoral agenda

Sectoral Programmes \ Intersecoral Themes	Regulatory Reform	Poverty	Environment	Social Development	Participation	Gender	Livelihoods	Human Rights
Housing	✓							✓
Water					✓			
Health		✓						
Education							✓	
Sanitation				✓	✓			
Transportation								

Linking practical and strategic objectives of programmes that are often difficult to engage within any one single actor – Whilst practical objectives are typically project based, and short term with relatively quick pay-offs, strategic objectives have a tendency to be policy based with longer term aims and impacts. Converging both practical and strategic agendas, essential for development work, demands partnerships between project based organizations (CBOs, NGOs, private contractors) and policy based organizations. (donors, governments). In the example of improving poor housing conditions, the practical agenda is often a lack of land and materials, inadequate credit, inappropriate design. The strategic agenda might include land tenure reform, rights of access and ownership, reducing dependency thinking, lack of security, lack of organizational capacity – all of which demand a shift in policy from providing, toward an enabling framework of legal and legislative reform *(see Figure 9)*.

Figure 9: Overlapping responsibilities create added complexity: shelter as an example

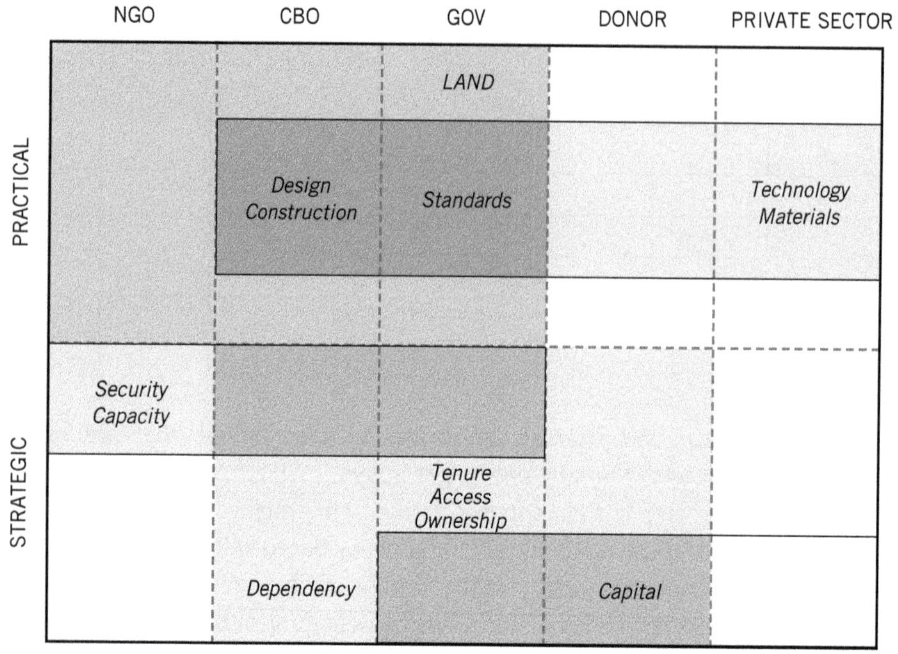

	NGO	CBO	GOV	DONOR	PRIVATE SECTOR
PRACTICAL			LAND		
		Design Construction	Standards		Technology Materials
	Security Capacity				
STRATEGIC			Tenure Access Ownership		
		Dependency		Capital	

◆ CHOOSING THE RIGHT PARTNERS

It is often said that "the partnership environment is less hostile if each partner sees a vested interest in the partnership." Understanding these vested interests – the conflicts and opportunities they offer for creative work – is both a prelude to effective participation and to partnership formation. In a similar way a knowledge of comparative advantage which actors bring to the partnership and the potential risk of their involvement needs evaluation.

Non-governmental organizations

Non governmental organizations (NGOs) distinguish themselves in various ways. For example, in their core ideology (their strong social bias or doctrine); their area of interest and work (environmental advocacy, children, disaster mitigation, relief); their function (project based, network based); their field of operation (local, regional, global); which in turn will define their core activities (community development, advocacy, project management, information dissemination, networking).

Each type of NGO will differ in their organizational identity (their mission or institutional goals), their technical and institutional capacity, their legal status, relations to government, management capability, and track records. NGO selection as a partner to development programmes whilst most times expedient (i.e. decided as much by political or cultural acceptability, availability or access to donor funds) will depend therefore on a careful assessment of the above.

Advantages/roles

NGOs bring grass roots knowledge and are flexible because of their independence from political or agency ties (see also *Risks* below). They can be relatively mobile given their horizontal and cellular structure. They bring knowledge and skill resources to which others may not have easy access (risk mitigation, technology, management experience). Their relative independence enables them often to innovate and to operate as mediators, building capacity for CBOs to become effective partners or entities in their own right. As partners they are often able to scale up work (connecting local organizations to each other – e.g. Waste Pickers, land rights organizations) and can command more trust than other partners. Their strong social bias enables them to focus on the poor and vulnerable, advocating their cause and place in governance.

Risks

More recently questions of legitimacy, accountability and cost-effectiveness have been raised in relation to NGO roles and responsibilities (Brinkerhoff, 2002:49, Edwards, 2000). In addition some have been criticised for adopting the core values of donors and becoming service contractors to the donor community. Donor appropriation either in terms of financial dependence or subscribing to donor priorities and rationale have undermined their advantages (Brinkerhoff, 2002:52). In response to donor demand some have changed their organizational structure (staff, routines, accountability) with the resultant loss of flexibility and independence. Short term objectives have often taken the place of longer term goals in the face of the need to develop a track record and fit into donor timetables.

Community-based organizations

Community-based organizations (CBOs) often represent discreet vested interest groups which cluster around a common cause, culture, practice or place. CBOs are not always representative of the broader community needs or interests, but rather are expedient partners for outsiders who may be seeking a community-based partner as demanded by donors. Often outsiders will engage those who are more organized, articulate or active. Communities, like NGOs, are really homogenous (indeed some are in open conflict with each other) and distinguish themselves in at least four ways: communities of interest (forming around land rights, eviction, security, clean water); communities of culture (sharing beliefs, language, ethnicity); communities of practice (sharing routines, information, markets, in relation to work); communities of place (people who may share a place – temporarily as in work or more permanently as in settlement). Effective community-based organizing will need to find representation across these different types of communities or indeed engage

NGOs bring grass roots knowledge and are flexible because of their independence from political or agency ties.

each separately as partners. In addition, representation will need to consider age, gender, disability, ethnicity. The search for a community partner may well need to begin by establishing links or local level partnerships *between* CBOs as a prelude to engaging a CBO with government, private sector organizations and others.

Advantages/roles
CBOs offer numerous advantages as partners. They are a good conduit to local beneficiaries in participatory programmes; they are often highly entrepreneurial and offer inventive ways of solving problems which might neither be available, or legitimate to more formal partners; they have a strong incentive to solve problems immediately – to keep the programme focused and on track; they bring local practical wisdom, accurate information, and low costs to the planning and implementation of programmes; they ensure compliance with social norms and facilitate access to local resources. Importantly, whilst these attributes offer a balanced assessment of comparative advantage, the selection of CBOs can often be based on a single criterion or desire – despite the fact the CBO itself may be neither legitimate or representative. For example, they may open doors to people or organizations and offer security for minority ethnic groups in the interests of longer term gains. In turn, CBOs often benefit from partnerships through a general improvement in the quality of life of their constituents, from the legitimacy or status brought to them by the partnership.

CBOs open doors and give access to people and knowledge often unavailable to others.

Risks
The engagement of CBOs in participatory development work holds various risks that may inhibit the full advantage of partnership work. For example, engagement with existing CBOs which may be expedient, may nevertheless reinforce existing leadership or social structures or elite groups which often are the very structures, which development programmes seek to disturb or change. A partnership may empower a CBO, leading to changes in the social dynamics of place and indeed violence.

When partnering with government organizations, CBOs like NGOs may find themselves distanced from their constituents. Over the longer term and given the financial and other resourced advantages which CBOs may accrue, dependency on other partners may develop, particularly with those who hold more power. In this case, CBOs may find their priorities shifting in compliance with these more powerful partners, negotiating votes for favours for example. In some cases CBOs will be seen less as partners as earlier defined and more as the implementation arm of outsiders, and may again lose their legitimacy and organizational identity (Brinkerhoff, 2002:55-6).

Government
As with other actors, government is composed of a cluster of organizations each often competing for power and resources., The focus here is more with

local government and with local level partnerships, although sometimes the military or the Port Authority will have influence on local decisions in cases where they own land or control access to land. All will have their own sets of vested interests (housing department, municipal works, education, health) – each seeking to measure their success quantitatively (houses built, water delivered, roads improved, health awareness raised) and qualitatively (improved livelihood, security, rights). Government represents a significant concentration of power which, in partnership, is often perceived to be threatening.

Advantages/roles
Government brings a number of comparative advantages which are essential and numerous. Underpinning all of these is the essential shift from a providing or lead role (building houses, centralising resources, standardising operations) to enabling and facilitating role (managing resources, decentralising resources, promoting variety and flexibility). Governments bring much needed service resources (administrative, research, training). In an enabling role they can promote social enterprise, provide a check on the dominance of elite groups, work as arbitrators, mediating between powerful stake holders, removing constraints which inhibit entrepreneurship, scale up programmes and establish enabling policies. For effective partnerships in the context of good governance, various criteria for engagement need consideration. There will be governments' ability to recognise its own limitations and to power share; the impact of inevitable inter-departmental competition; the need quite often to meet donor demands or international criteria for loans (structural adjustment for example) which may take precedent over local or national priorities. There will be a need to modify their prejudice about community and NGO competence, especially in politically or culturally uncertain contexts. In addition there will be the governments' track record vis-a-vis corruption and their susceptibility to change in politically volatile settings which may disrupt the continuity of programmes (Brinkerhoff, 2002:59-60).

Risks
It has often been argued that government authorities' engagement with civil society groups can help reinforce political polarities which are sometimes a threat to good governance. In addition, participation with CBOs can often generate wish lists of wants and needs which raises expectations amongst community groups and which, if government cannot meet them will threaten their viability and electability. Risks for government may include the diversion of funds to NGOs and CBOs over whom government will have less control and which may encourage the more skilled to move away from government and into the non-government sector. Finally, there will be a risk to the community of being co-opted by government given past experience and so serving the needs and priorities of government authorities rather than their own constituencies.

In an enabling role governments can promote social enterprise, check on the dominance of elite groups and work as arbiters.

Donors

All donors, whether multilateral or bilateral, will have signed up to the Millennium Development Goals. However, their priorities will differ according to their own political needs, their strengths and bias. For example, rural versus urban focus or technically versus socially driven programmes), their own regional areas of cultural or political interest which are usually historically established, and the needs and priorities of that region as may be negotiated with national governments. Donors will wield significant power given their resources and will sometimes tie their aid to securing partners who serve their interests best and with least risk.

Advantages/roles
Donors pool significant resources of knowledge and case experience that they pass on in various ways, including through technical assistance programmes and knowledge dissemination. They are sometimes able to scale up programmes more effectively than national governments. Donors often partner universities and research institutes to undertake research and innovate with new methods, technologies, tools and ideas. Donors are well placed to bring people and organizations together with proper representation and to ensure that the Millennium Development Goals are prioritised in development programmes

Risks
In view of their size and their national mandate, donors can be inflexible and will seek clear outputs despite changes that might occur during the programme development stages. Staff turnover will generally be high. Experience in some regions has shown that donor involvement in restructuring national economies, or democratising governments according to donor's norms, can be socially destabilising and can even threaten national sovereignty.

Private corporate sector

The private corporate sector (including both nationals and multinationals) plays an increasingly significant role as a partner in development programmes, recognising that its own self-interests are best served when it combines corporate interests with an equivalent corporate social responsibility. Corporate philanthropy has grown significantly, with multinationals in some cases establishing their own foundations, directing research into socially and environmentally sustainable ways in which their programmes might be structured.

Advantages/roles
The private sector brings substantial technical, organizational and entrepreneurial skills to a partnership (marketing, forecasting, research).

> *Donors pool significant resources that they pass on in various ways.*

Private sector organizations open doors to a wide network of enterprises, especially the national and multinationals.

They offer employment to local markets, investment opportunity to national enterprises, and innovations in technology and management. Private sector organizations open doors to a wide network of enterprises especially the national and multinationals. They are pragmatic and performance-related. Their contribution to development and not just business can improve relationships with local partners and the international development community, which can reduce risk to their enterprise and maximise profits.

Risks

Private sector partnerships with government authorities will often be over-regulated, inhibiting flexibility and entrepreneurship. They will often face hostility from civil society groups in view of their track record on employment and wages to local women, children and others, and on environmentally irresponsible practices. The private sector, whilst accustomed to long-term planning, will often seek short-term results that may not fit longer-term development goals of development agencys or governments. When partnering with local NGOs or CBOs they risk entanglement in local politics or conflicts, which will undermine their ability to meet targets. Finally, development objectives can often distract or even demotivate employees from their core business, which in turn can undermine the efficiency of the organization (Brinkerhoff, 2002:70).

◆ BUILDING PARTNERSHIPS

We have so far seen the need for clarity about the vested interests of partners, as well as the advantages and risks that they will bring to partnership arrangements. We have also seen how the purpose of partnership, one way or another, is to build organizational capacity – to pool resources in order to meet common objectives. When building partnerships three issues need further consideration: partnership types (what kind serves our purpose?), partnership capacities (who should we partner with and how do we decide), and levels of operation.

Partnership types

In common practice, there are 3 types of operational partnerships identified:

Associative partnerships

This is where an association is negotiated in pursuit of specific aims – a deal with the municipality over land rights or land sharing, for example. Once the specific aims have been met, the partnership dissolves. It is temporary, output related and often short-term.

Partnership entities
This occurs where an organization is formed which has a 'centre' often place based and often with some sense of formal (even hierarchical) decision making structure. Examples include saving societies, housing co-operatives or re-cycling enterprises. Partnership entities will often begin as associative (for example between communities threatened with eviction) who may subsequently emerge as an entity (a saving society for the purchase then management and maintenance of their new settlement). Entities will seek to survive beyond their initial mandate, are transformative and adaptable to a wider agenda of ideals or objectives. For example, a savings society builds commitment and solidarity as well as serves to empower the community whilst saving money to meet practical needs. Partnership entities may network with other entities who share values and objectives and become, in time, a network organization.

Partnership networks
Networks arise where organizations, often with grass root interests, gain power and authority as part of a larger collective, citywide, in order to influence decisions, secure rights, gain access to services. These networks can operate nationally, for example, Muungano wa Wanavijiji (Federation of Slum Dwellers) in Kenya; SPARC (Society for the Promotion of Area Resource Centres) in India and People's Dialogue in South Africa), regionally (for example, ACHR– Asian Coalition for Housing Rights), or internationally (for example, SDI (Slum/Shack Dwellers International) and environmental or fair trade lobby groups). Network organizations tend to be less hierarchical and more egalitarian in structure and non- place based. They may represent communities of interest, practice, culture, or combinations of these. Their objectives will often be practical (better sanitation, adequate shelter) and strategic (rights, governance, etc).

A pioneering study on partnership types distinguished four categories of partnerships according to primary purpose and degree of power-sharing (Rodal and Mulder, 1993, cited in TBS, 1998):

(i) *consultative* – to obtain relevant input for developing policies and strategies, and for programme/service design, delivery, evaluation and adjustment.

(ii) *contributory* – to leverage new resources or funds for program/ service delivery.

(iii) *operational* – to permit partners to share resources and work, and exchange information for programme/service delivery.

(iv) *collaborative* – to encourage joint decision-taking with regard to policy development, strategic planning, and programme/service design, delivery, evaluation and adjustment.

The above categories are not always discrete. The various modes of partnering may be cumulative (for example, a collaborative arrangement could also be consultative, contributory and operational) or a particular arrangement may evolve over time from one category to another (Demirjian, 2002).

Partnership capabilities
(who should we partner with and how do we decide?)

One of the key reasons why projects fail, or indeed have difficulty in getting started, is the lack of capacity to deliver and then to sustain programmes. Lack of commitment or interest and overly ambitious objectives are two further reasons. Similarly, the success of partnership arrangements is very often contingent on finding the right partner and ensuring that the partners' identities are maintained and their interests met. Two sets of activities are therefore key when deciding appropriate partners.

Selection Criteria

This involves developing acceptable and realistic criteria for making choices. The criteria themselves are only a guide. The final choice will often also be affected by political expediency, partner availability and financial feasibility.

Table 4: Things to consider when choosing partners

	NGO	CBO	Government	Donor	Private Sector
Political viability					
Track record					?
Corruption					
Political will					
Capacity					
Compatibility	?				
Experience					
Commitment			?		
Reputation					
Resources					
Representativeness					
Legitimacy					
Transparency					
Credibility					
Status					

Table 5: Factors for success and characteristics of failed partnership

Factors for success that have emerged from surveys of partnerships and workshops of practitioners involved in creating and running partnerships, and characteristics of failed attempts at partnership, or warnings that something is going wrong

Successful partnership	Failed partnership
• Agreement that a partnership is necessary.	• A history of conflict among key interests.
• Respect and trust between different interests.	• One partner manipulates or dominates.
• The leadership of a respected individual or individuals.	• Lack of clear purpose.
• Commitment of key interests developed through a clear and open process.	• Unrealistic goals.
• The development of a shared vision of what might be achieved.	• Differences of philosophy and ways of working.
• Time to build the partnership.	• Lack of communication.
• Shared mandates or agendas.	• Unequal and unacceptable balance of power and control.
• The development of compatible ways of working, and flexibility.	• Key interests missing from the partnership.
• Good communication, perhaps aided by a facilitator.	• Hidden agendas.
• Collaborative decision-making, with a commitment to achieving consensus.	• Financial and time commitments outweigh the potential benefits.
• Effective organizational management.	

Source: Partnerships Online http://www.partnerships.org.uk/AZP/part.html

Stakeholder analysis of interests and capacities

In any partnership each of the principal actors will either be primary, secondary, or external stakeholders *(See Table 6)*. Primary stakeholders, whether CBOs, Private Sector Organisations or Government Authorities, will be those directly effected by any project or programme. Secondary stakeholders will usually be intermediaries who may be NGOs or governments, through whom funds may be channelled or

Part 2 Partnerships in Action

who may be acting as mediators between, for example, CBOs and Municipal Authorities. External stakeholders are those who may provide funds, human resources or technical information but will not normally have a local presence – for example, donors, multilaterals operating through foundations.

All stakeholders will have an interest in the programme. All will have their own priorities that will often need to be negotiated and converged. During the course of this stakeholder analysis it will be assumed that not all parties will hold equal power. The ability of each to persuade or coerce others will therefore need to be assessed and the positive and negative impacts on any course of action carefully considered. *Table 6* below illustrates.

Table 6: Stakeholder analysis

	Interests	Priority of Interests	Influence/Impact on Project (+) (−)
Primary stakeholders			
Secondary stakeholders			
External stakeholders			

Whilst the above chart offers a broad assessment of the interests and priorities of the stakeholders it may sometimes be necessary to explore in more depth the motivation and likely participation of specific actor groups. *Figure 10* below and *Table 7* illustrate the characteristics of different sets of community groups, as an example.

Figure 10: Spatial relation of communities and participatory partners.

The **Inner ring** contains structured communities who make ideal participatory partners, but also contains transitory communities with little cohesion and with the highest needs.

The **Outer ring** contains structured communities who are more reluctant as participatory partners. Squatter communities are also found, who vary from ideal to transitory.

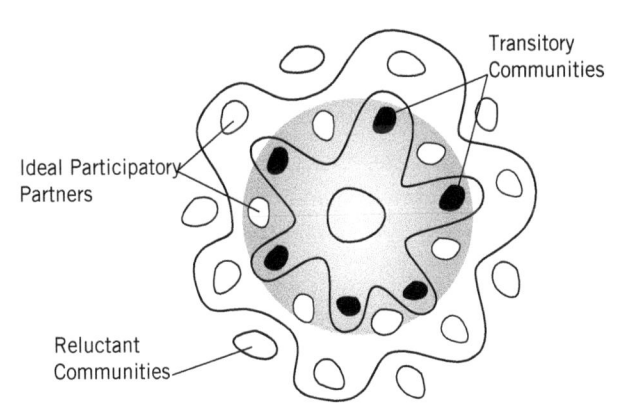

Source: Action Planning for Cities, Hamdi & Goethert

SCHEMATIC URBAN PATTERN

Table 7: Characteristics of communities as participatory partners

Type of Community	Characteristics	Appropriate Tool
IDEAL PARTICIPATORY PARTNERS: Cohesive, highly organized, lower income	• Much to gain; supports their needs and assists in long term stabilisation • Easiest in terms of effort	• Community Action • ZOPP • Planning for real
TRANSITORY COMMUNITIES: Non-cohesive, transitory	• Much to gain; but need organizing; action planning starts stabilising community • Requires much effort; customary target of community development inputs	• Community Action Planning • Planning for real
RELUCTANT COMMUNITIES: Cohesive, highly organized, higher income	• Little to gain; already in the power system • Difficult to work with: may not need workshops since already access to power and experts come from this strata: they can use the direct or consultative level of participation with sufficient confidence to reflect community income	• Urban Community Assistance Team

Source: Hamdi & Goethert, Action Planning for Cities, n.d.

Stakeholder analysis is best conducted in workshop format if possible. It is an integral part of the action planning process highlighted below. Where workshops are not possible, a self-assessment of stakeholder interests, influences and priorities is highly recommended as a basis for convergence and partnership formation.

Partnership levels

Each of our actor categories (NGOs, CBOs etc.) will operate at a variety of levels within the spectrum of planning decisions. *Table 8* on the right disaggregates these into constituencies and levels.

Part 2 *Partnerships in Action*

Table 8: Actors and levels

		PARTNERS		
		State	*Market*	*Community*
LEVELS	*Local/Urban*	Local authorities Municipalities	Formal and informal small-scale enterprises and service providers and utilities	CBOs; communities of place, culture, practice, interest, resistance
	Regional/ National	Central Government and Departments (Housing, Health, Education, etc.)	National level enterprises (transportation, utilities, manufacturers)	Network organizations and federations
	Global	UN and other bilateral and multilateral organizations (donors, trade organizations)	Multinationals	Advocacy groups, unions, global networks

Figure 11: Actors and levels

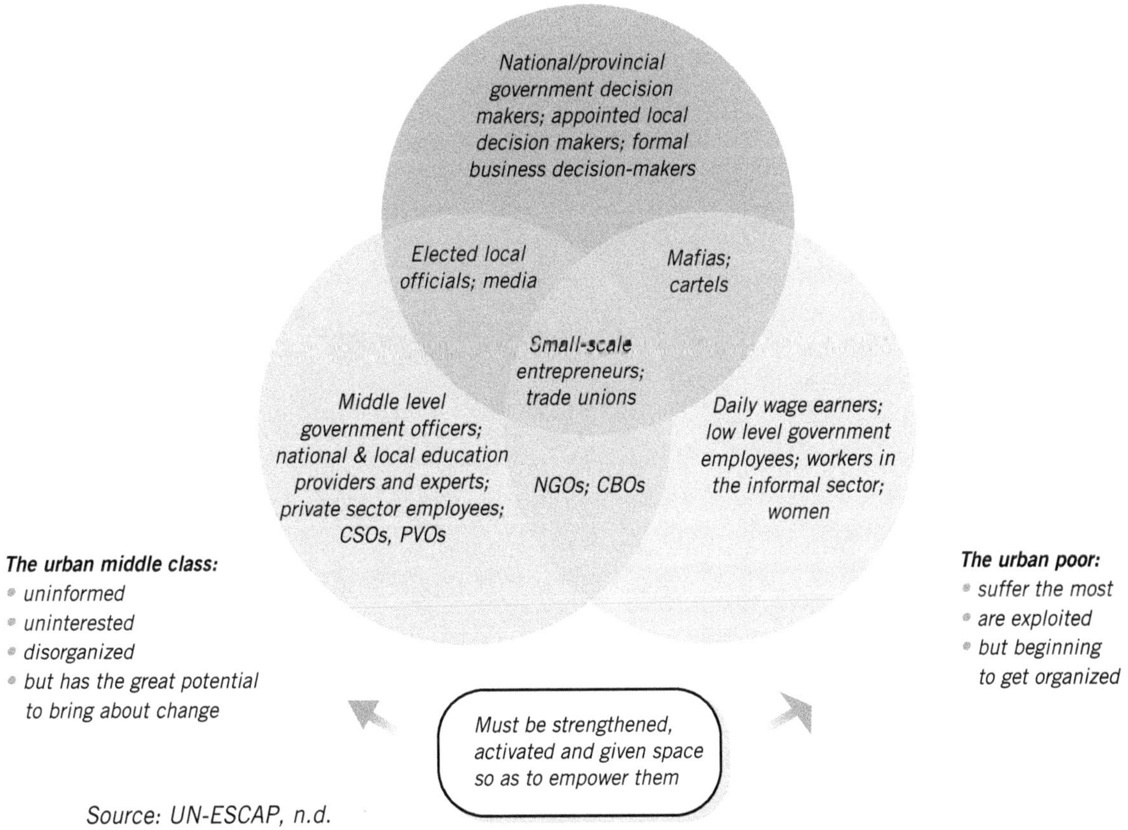

National/provincial government decision makers; appointed local decision makers; formal business decision-makers

Elected local officials; media

Mafias; cartels

Small-scale entrepreneurs; trade unions

Middle level government officers; national & local education providers and experts; private sector employees; CSOs, PVOs

NGOs; CBOs

Daily wage earners; low level government employees; workers in the informal sector; women

The urban middle class:
- uninformed
- uninterested
- disorganized
- but has the great potential to bring about change

The urban poor:
- suffer the most
- are exploited
- but beginning to get organized

Must be strengthened, activated and given space so as to empower them

Source: UN-ESCAP, n.d.

43

Part 2 Partnerships in Action

Figure 12: Actors and levels

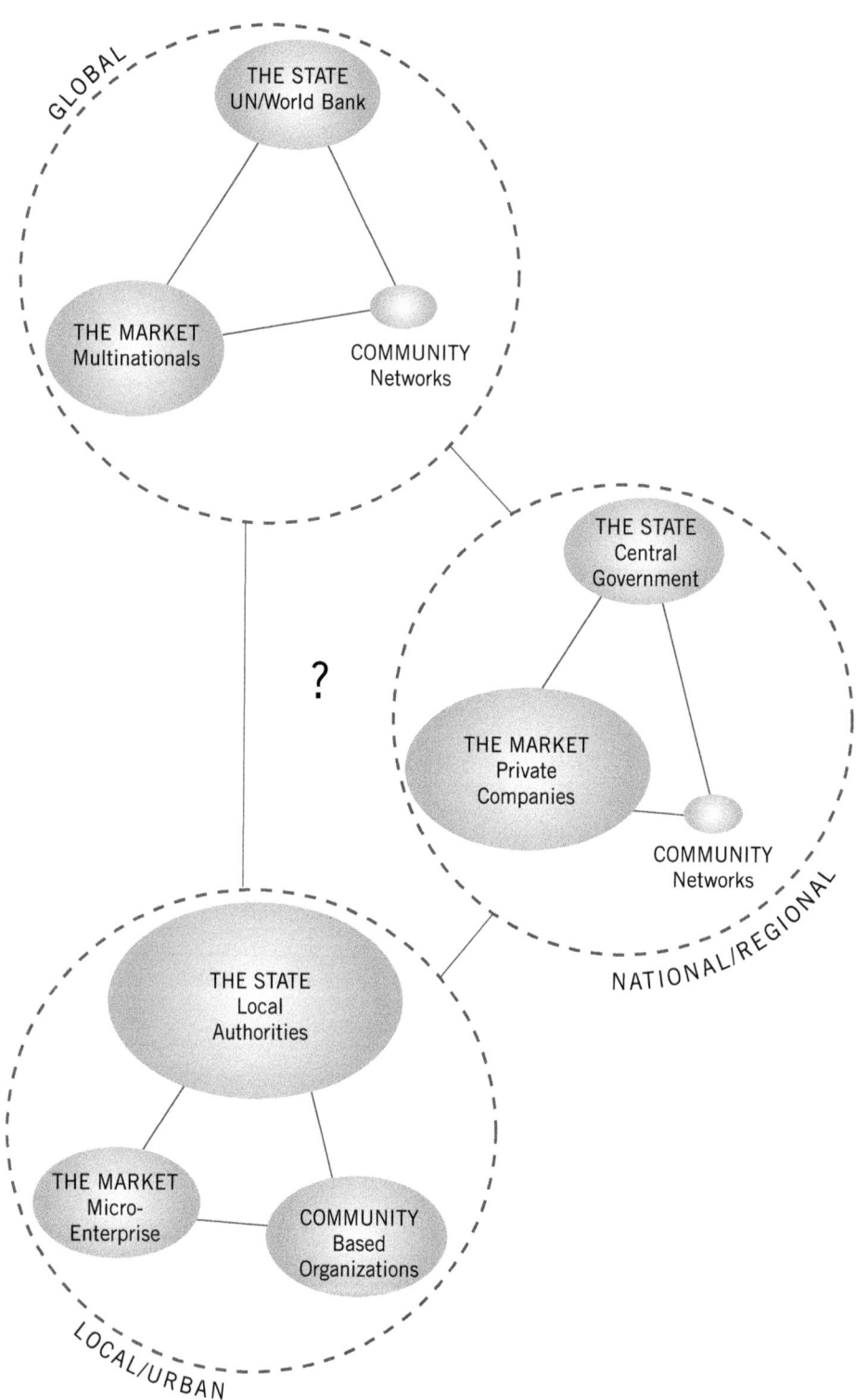

Figure 12 illustrates the triadic relationship between the state, the market and the community at local/urban, national/regional, and international levels. This raises a number of further questions when it comes to partnership formation. For example, what might the form and value be of partnerships between communities and networks at the local, national and global levels? Or, between small entrepreneurs and informal traders at the local level with private sector partners at the national level, or corporations at the global level? Are there linkages and relationships that have yet to be explored in the interests of good global governance and what qualitative form might these take? What capacitates and who should provide these will be needed at the local/urban level for communities and informal traders to become partners nationally, even globally.

◆ ACTION PLANNING – REACHING CONSENSUS

Good partnerships, indeed successful participatory programmes, begin when actors come together to achieve a common goal based on agreed priorities, pooling resources and maximising comparative advantage. Action planning methods can be effective in achieving these aims, securing partnerships based on stakeholder interests and between the various levels of actors identified in *Table 8*. Action planning typically includes the following groups of activity: (Hamdi and Goethert, 1997)

- identifying problems and opportunities
- setting goals and priorities
- deciding options and tradeoffs
- establishing resources and defining constraints
- forming project teams and allocating tasks
- implementing and monitoring projects and programmes.

The process begins with identifying problems in a manner that avoids apportioning blame – and with identifying opportunities. Problem solving will depend on problem finding. The initial list of problems may well be a wish list of favourite laments (we must stop squatters) or slogans of politicians (provide water for all). It is also likely that problems which may be high on the agenda of one party will have no resonance for another (e.g. increased co-ordination, lower standards, preservation of aquifers, which will be important for planners, will not feature as significant for communities).

Analysis at this stage will focus on clarity with four objectives in mind: to avoid pre-conceptions about solutions; to observe where there is already consensus about issues and therefore a clue to partnership formation; to flag potentially conflicting demands which may undermine potential partnerships; and to understand issues that seem to be differences but are actually similarities when expressed or interpreted in different ways. In all respects, the need here is to position problems well enough in order to converge the interests of actors in pursuit of appropriate solutions.

Progressive definition of problems, prioritised, interpreted and positioned according to cause and effect (why is it a problem and to whom), is a basis to from which to set goals – what do we need, what resources do we have, what can we build on, what can we realistically expect to achieve? Goals are prioritised according to need and then ranked according to feasibility. Alternative strategies are worked out for how to get what is needed, and again prioritised according to urgency, desirability and feasibility. For each option we devise, we give some consideration to the risks involved, the investment entailed, the commitment demanded, and the likely constraints to be encountered. How likely is it for example that we will get what we want if we ask for a new school building and who or what is likely to get in our way? Does it meet the needs of all partners? How much money will it entail and what investment of time and energy? Constraints are analysed in terms of what or who will get in the way of getting projects going, which will typically include institutional, financial, technical, environmental or political hurdles, which will have to be overcome. Once identified, ideas and procedures for overcoming hurdles are brainstormed – who can help, how and when. Realistic projects are identified – those that can start sooner rather than later – and then analysed in terms of their resource demands, the capacities inherent in each of the actor groups as well as their relative dependences and inter-dependency.

Progressive definitions of problems, prioritised, interpreted and positioned according to cause and effect (why is it a problem and to whom) is a basis to goal setting.

During the final phase of planning, project teams are formed and a plan of action is devised and phased with timetables, costs, commitments and responsibilities. "Whilst these projects (initially) may be ill-conceived, uncoordinated, technically naïve, or fragmented ...... they represent development avenues behind which the desire to implement is manifested" (Baross, 1991). They represent a basis around which people and organizations can partner and participate. These kinds of action plans also serve importantly to offer an early insight into the organizational capabilities of the communities, to the responsiveness of planners and government authorities, the potential for partnership and the resistance of those in charge to change and adapt. They are vehicles for learning and identifying institutional capabilities and training needs as much as for solving problems. They offer a basis in which to organize communities and build their capacity to become effective partners in governance. In this way the action plan not only serves practical needs on the ground but also important strategic functions, which can influence policy and ensure local level participation in the governance of cities (Hamdi and Goethert, 1997:44 – 51).

PART 3 Guiding Principles

- Understand power relations, comparative advantage and the vested interests of actors as a prelude to partnership formation.

- Safeguard the poor and vulnerable in partnership formation, given that power relations are never equal.

- Decide the most suitable type of partnership – consultative, contributory, operational, collaborative – in relation to purpose: scaling up, securing access to resources, promoting good governance, de-centralisation etc.

- Decide the kind of organization to which the partnership will lead (associative, network, entity) in pursuit of purpose.

- Ensure partnerships create and maintain organizational identity based on shared commitments, mission, and core values, whilst safeguarding the distinctive identity of individual partners.

- Sort out levels of partner relations (local/urban, national/regional, global) in pursuit of both practical and strategic agendas.

- Understand partnership capacities through a stakeholder analysis and determine interests and priorities as a basis to partner selection.

- Assess the advantages of participation and partnership in meeting the stated purpose and evaluate risk in relation to opportunities.

- Utilise participatory action planning methods in order to converge the interests of stakeholders and pool resources for project and programme design, implementation and management.

References

Ashley, C. and D. Carney (1999) *Sustainable Livelihoods: Lessons from Early Experience*. Department for International Development, London

Baharoglu, D. and C. Kessides (n.d.) *Urban Poverty*. http://poverty.worldbank.org/files/4418_chap16.pdf

Baross, P. (1991) *Action Planning, Working Paper No. 2*. Institute for Housing and Urban, Development Studies, Rotterdam

Bonfiglioli, A. (n.d.) *'Empowering the poor: UNCDF's contribution to poverty reduction and local governance'*. http://unpan1.un.org/intradoc/groups/public/documents/un/unpan010166.pdf

Boyle, R. (n.d.) *Partnership within ADAPT: A study*. www.adapt.leargas.ie/download/Partner.rtf

Brinkerhoff J.M. (2002) *Partnership for International Development: Rhetoric or Results?* Boulder, Lynne Rienner Publishers

Buch-Hansen, E. (2002) *Are partnership and participation "magic wands" for promoting sustainability, democratisation, equity and poverty reduction?* www.cdr.dk/aidimpactforum/papers/Participation%20AIF%20oplaeg%2029-10-02.pdf

CARE International UK (2001) *Participation, policy and urban poverty*. CARE International

Demirjian, A. (2002) *Partnering in Support of International Development Initiatives: The INTOSAI Case Study*. www.sti.ch/pdfs/swap318.pdf

DPU (Development Planning Unit) (2001) *Implementing the Habitat Agenda: In Search of Urban Sustainability*. DPU, London

Drakakis-Smith, D. (1996) *Third World cities: sustainable urban development*, in R. Paddison, B. Lever and J. Money (Eds) *International Perspectives in Urban Studies 4*. Jessica Kingsley Publishers, London

Edwards, M. (2000) *NGO Rights and Responsibilities*. The Foreign Policy Centre, London

Frank, F. and A. Smith (2000) *The Partnership Handbook*. www.seda.sk.ca/pdfs/HRDCpartnerhdbk.pdf

Garau, P. and E.D. Sclar (2004) *Interim Report of the Task Force 8 on Improving the Lives of Slum. Executive Summary*. www.unmillenniumproject.org/documents/tf8interim.pdf

Gilbert, R., D. Stevenson, H. Girardet and R. Stren (1996) *Making Cities Work: The Role of Local Authorities in the Urban Environment*. Earthscan, London

Halla, F. (2002) *Participatory Approaches to Urban Planning in Tanzania*.

Hamdi, N. and R. Goethert (1997) *Action Planning for Cities*. John Wiley and Sons, Chicester

Hardoy, Jorge E., Mitlin and Satterthwaite (2001) *Environmental Problems in an Urbanizing World: Finding Solutions for Cities in Africa, Asia and Latin America.* Earthscan, London

Hassan, A. and R. Zetter (2002) *Sustainable development: between development and environment agendas in the developing world* in R. Zetter and R. White (eds) *Planning in Cities: Sustainability and Growth in the Developing World.* ITDG Publishing, London

Hinrichsen, D., R.M. Salem and R. Blackburn (2002) *Meeting the Urban Challenge. Population Reports.* Series M, No. 16. Baltimore, The Johns Hopkins Bloomberg School of Public Health, Population Information Program, Fall 2002
http://www.unmillenniumproject.org/documents/tf8interim%20execsum.pdf

Hussein, K. (2002) *Livelihoods Approaches Compared: A Multi-Agency Review of Current Practice.* Department for International Development, London and Overseas Development Institute, London, www.livelihoods.org/info/docs/LAC.pdf

Ibanda, S. (2003) *Participatory Approaches to Urban Planning: Ugandan Case Study.*
(Available on accompanying CD-ROM)

ITDG–EA (2001b) *Kitale Community Based Planning Tool Kit.*
(Available on accompanying CD-ROM)

ITDG–EA (2001c) *Kitale Scan Survey Summary Report.*
(Available on accompanying CD-ROM)

ITDG–EA (2002a) *Community-based organizations (CBOs)/associations inventory and household poverty survey report – Kitale Municipality.*
(Available on accompanying CD-ROM)

ITDG–EA (2002d) *Kipsongo Neighbourhood Plan.*
(Available on accompanying CD-ROM)

ITDG–EA (2002e) *Kipsongo: Summary of Planning Issues.*
(Available on accompanying CD-ROM)

ITDG–EA (2002f) *Shimo La Tewa Neighbourhood Plan.*
(Available on accompanying CD-ROM)

ITDG–EA (2002g) 'Survey Report on Tuwan Estate'
(Available on accompanying CD-ROM)

ITDG–EA (2003) *Building in Partnership: Participatory Urban Planning International Workshop, 9-12 June 2003, Kitale, Kenya: Workshop Report.*
(Available on accompanying CD-ROM)

Jahan, S. (2003) *Achieving Millennium Development Goals: Partnership and participation.* www.icnrd5-mongolia.mn/papers/paper8.doc

Jaura, R. (2001) *Berlin Conference Pledges Sustainable Development of Cities.* Inter Press Service, www.globalpolicy.org/socecon/confrnce/urban21.htm

Leyland, T. (1991) *Participation in the 80's and 90's: Who asks the questions? MSc dissertation.* Unpublished MSc dissertation, University of Edinburgh
www.eldis.org/fulltext/leyland.pdf

LIFE (Local Initiative Facility for Urban Environment) (1997) *Participatory Local Governance: LIFE's Method and Experience 1992–1997.* Technical Advisory Paper 1

Lyons, M. (2004) *Building in Partnership: Participatory Urban Planning (BIP-PUP) End-of Project Evaluation, 7-15 March, 2004.*
(Available on accompanying CD-ROM).

Mabogunje, A. L. (2003) *Access to Basic Services in African Local Governments: Understanding the Challenge and Starting Action,* Paper presented at Africities Summit, Yaounde , Cameroon, 2 – 6 December 2003, Ensuring access to basic services in African local governments

McGranahan, G. and D. Satterthwaite (2002) *Environmental health or ecological sustainability? Reconciling the brown and green agendas in urban development* in R. Zetter and R. White (Eds) *Planning in Cities: Sustainability and Growth in the Developing World.* ITDG Publishing, London

Oakley, P. et al. (1991) *Projects with People: The Practice of Participation in Rural Development.* International Labour Organization, Geneva

Peil, M. (1994) *Urban housing and services in Anglophone West Africa: coping with an inadequate environment* in H. Main, Hamish and S. W. Williams (Eds) *Environment and Housing in Third World Cities.* John Wiley and Sons, Chichester

Poole, D.L. (1995) *Partnerships buffer and strengthen.* Health and Social Work 20(1), pp. 2-5.

PRC (Population Resource Center) (2001) *Briefing: Globalization and Urbanization: U.S. Health and Security Concerns.* www.prcdc.org/programs/monterey/monterey.html

Ríos, S.B. de los and S.T Yáñez (n.d.) 'Case Study: *Participatory Planning in La Ensenada Valley, Puente Piedra District, Lima.* (Available on accompanying CD-ROM)

Ruskulis, O. (2002a) *Participatory Urban Planning: Literature and Current Knowledge Review.* (Available on accompanying CD-ROM)

Ruskulis, O. (2002b) *Review of Literature and Current Knowledge on Participatory Planning, Particularly in the Context Of Informal Settlement Development.*
(Available on accompanying CD-ROM)

Ruskulis, O. (2002c) *Summary: Review of Existing Knowledge on Participatory Planning in Urban Development.* (Available on accompanying CD-ROM)

Saha, S. R. and R. Habibur (2003) *Case study (Bangladesh part) on Building in partnership: participatory urban planning.* (Available on accompanying CD-ROM)

SURF-AS (Sub-regional Resource Facility for Arab States) (1999) *Participatory development: risks and & conditions for success.*
www.surfas.org/Papers/participatory.pdf

TBS (Treasury Board of Canada Secretariat) (1998) *Alternative Service Delivery: Citizen-Centred Service and the Partnership Option.*
www.tbs-sct.gc.ca/asd-dmps/pubs/toc_e.asp

UN (United Nations), (2004) *World Urbanization Prospects The 2003 Revision: Data Tables and Highlights.* www.un.org/esa/population/publications/wup2003/2003WUPHighlights.pdf

UNCED (United Nations Conference on Environment and Development) (1992) *Agenda 21 and other UNCED Agreements*. www.igc.apc.org/habitat/agenda21/

UNCHS (United Nations Centre for Human Settlements [Habitat]) (1994) *Population, Urbanization and Quality of Life*. UNCHS (Habitat) contribution to the International Conference on Population and Development, (1994), UNCHS (Habitat), Nairobi

UNCHS (United Nations Centre for Human Settlements [Habitat]) (1997) *The Istanbul Declaration and Habitat Agenda*. UNCHS (Habitat), Nairobi

UNCHS (United Nations Centre for Human Settlements [Habitat]) (2001b) *The State of the World's Cities 2001*. UNCHS (Habitat), Nairobi

UNCHS United Nations Centre for Human Settlements [Habitat]) (2001a) *Urban Millennium: Everyone deserves a decent place to live* www.unchs.org/ Istanbul+5/brochure.pdf

UNDP (n.d.) *Sustainable Urban Livelihoods Concept Paper (Draft)*. www.undp.org/s

UNDP (United Nations Development Programme) (1998) *Empowering people: A guidebook to participation*. www.undp.org/csopp/CSO/NewFiles/docemppeople.html

UN-ESCAP (United Nations Economic and Social Commission for Asia and the Pacific) (n.d.) *What is Good Governance?* www.unescap.org/huset/gg/governance.htm

UN-Habitat (2003) *Guide to Monitoring Target 11: Improving the lives of 100 million slum dwellers*. www.unhabitat.org/programmes/guo/documents/mdgtarget11.Pdf

UN-Habitat (n.d.) *Best Practice Briefs: Urban governance practices*. http://bestpractices.org/bpbriefs/Urban_Governance.html

UN-Habitat (United Nations Human Settlements Programme) and UNEP (United Nations Environment Programme) (2002) *Sustainable Cities Programme 1990–2000: A decade of United Nations Support for Broad-based Participatory Management of Urban Development*

World Bank (2003) *World Development Report 2003: Sustainable Development In A Dynamic World: Transforming Institutions, Growth, And Quality Of Life*. www.dynamicsustainabledevelopment.org/showsection.php?file=TOC.htm

World Bank (2004) *Partnerships in development: Progress in the fight against poverty*. The International Bank for Reconstruction and Development/The World Bank, Washington, DC http://poverty.worldbank.org/files/15028_wb_partners.pdf

Yahya, S. (2002) *The Origins of Participatory Planning in Kenya*. (Available on accompanying CD-ROM)

Zetter, R. (2002) *Market enablement or sustainable development: the conflicting paradigms of urbanization* in R. Zetter and R. White (Eds) *Planning in Cities: Sustainability and Growth in the Developing World*. ITDG Publishing, London

Online Resources

Empowering People: A Guide to Participation www.undp.org/sl/Documents/Manuals/Empowering/toc.htm

Participation Home Page
http://www.ids.ac.uk/ids/particip/

Participation in International Development - some quick links to resource documents
http://www.ipeople.cwc.net/Pages/iPiSDipql.htm

Partnerships and Participation in Planning
http://www.uap.vt.edu/cdrom/default.htm

Partnerships online – Partnerships and Participation
http://www.partnerships.org.uk/

Resource Book on Participation
http://www.iadb.org/exr/english/POLICIES/participate/index.htm

The Community Planning Website
http://www.communityplanning.net/

The World Bank Participation and Civic Engagement Website
http://www.worldbank.org/participation/

The World Bank Participation Sourcebook
http://www.worldbank.org/wbi/sourcebook/sbhome.htm

Tools to Support Participatory Urban Decision Making
http://www.unhabitat.org/cdrom/governance/html/cover.htm

Notes

www.ingramcontent.com/pod-product-compliance
Ingram Content Group UK Ltd.
Pitfield, Milton Keynes, MK11 3LW, UK
UKHW050523150426
5217IPUK00026B/1761